Super Crazy Fun

PRESCHOOL PHONICS

WARNING!

Lots of crazy words!

This textbook came about as the result of 20 years of trying to make kids enjoy learning English. It is designed around the use of the rhotic R and other characteristics of English pronunciation common in North America. We believe it can be used in other parts of the world as most phonics books can, and we are keen to hear feedback from anyone who tries this.

We want to make clear that the word "crazy" used in the title is in relation to any of the common definitions illustrated below, and does not refer in any way to the meaning "insane."

strange/illogical

wild

unexpected   **fun**

unwise

About the Authors:

Matthew Hitch has taught English in Korea for the better part of 20 years and holds a master's degree in applied linguistics. He clearly does not have a pig nose, and by most accounts is not at all malodorous. He also cuts a dashing figure according to his wife.

Sunok Moon prefers to go by the name Michelle, and is in fact quite scary as reported in the bio on the back of this book. She has a degree in English literature and has taught English in Korea for approximately 3 weeks longer than Matthew, who is writing this and finds it weird to refer to himself in the third person.

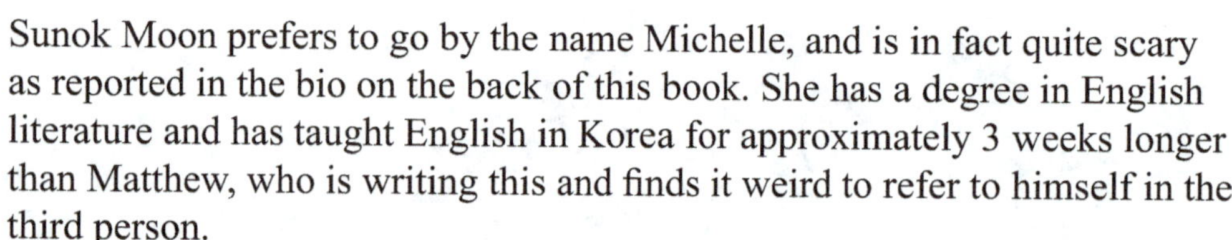

Contents

Welcome parents and teachers!

Thank you for considering our book. Phonics books are notoriously boring, so this is the last bastion of publishing where even the tiniest bit of creativity can raise the bar (sorry phonics book publishers, but it's true). With that said, we humbly offer you our content. We have also intentionally challenged convention in a few ways. Much of what we have to say may be used or discarded though, and these books can be used just like any other mainstream phonics book. We hope you will choose to use whatever you please and dispose of the rest.

Please allow us to explain just where our method of teaching phonics may diverge from mainstream approaches, and please do forgive us for sharing information from what is undeniably the most mind-numbingly boring and seemingly useless field of study, linguistics. Most phonics books are not written by scholars in the field of linguistics. They are mostly written by early childhood educators, so perhaps that's the first divergence. We'll start with how we sound out consonants. In linguistic studies it is not uncommon for consonants to be distinguished by using a vowel (usually "ah") on both sides. This means a "V" sounds like "ahvah" and an "F" sounds like "ahfah" and so on. Most phonics books distinguish consonant sounds without such preceding vowel, but they do follow with a vowel in the form of the schwa. This is fine for most consonants, but the ones that are able to be maintained until breath is exhausted can be confusing with a schwa where they end a word. It's mostly ESL students who feel this confusion, but we think it doesn't hurt to teach those consonants without a schwa to native speakers as well, so where "V" sounds like "və" in most phonics books, in our book it is presented as "vvvvvvv" with no schwa. We apply this to all long consonant sounds in our audio files (L,M,N&R are also presented as long with a tiny schwa sound at the end though). If you have read this far, we take our hats off to you. Most would be fast asleep by now.

The next divergence is our use of Magic E. We chose Magic E for the fun potential. The Split Digraphs just can't seem to hold a crowd. Magic E is no longer used in most educational settings for many reasons, but mostly because as a rule it cannot be defined clearly. We do mention that split digraphs are better though, mainly to extend an olive branch to all the teachers we hope will buy our books.

And the final divergence we would like to mention is our choice of words. Our choice of words may seem a bit odd at times throughout the books, but we chose them for their potential for keeping kids engaged over their usefulness. We approach a phonics book as a tool to teach about sounds much more than vocabulary. Poop, vomit, spit, fart, snot, and burp are the most popular with our students. We tried to find a spot for booger, but alas...

Our word choice is also strange in that it includes words that have the long E vowel when teaching split digraphs. Most phonics books glance over the long E vowel. The argument we have heard for this is that it is difficult for the younger students, but we suspect that it's avoided more because it's difficult for authors to find suitable words. We decided to give it a try, and our experience is that the long E words we chose are not that difficult for our students to grasp. Given that English is their second language, we believe native English speaking kids will cope with them just fine. Also you may notice our sight words are not all actually sight words - oops! Anyway, we hope you enjoy our silly books.

Welcome students!

Our friend E has a cool trick!
He can make his friends
A, E, I, O, and U say their names!

We call him Magic E!

It looks like fun, so we made a
rule that he is allowed to do it
if he wants to!

This is Magic E rule!

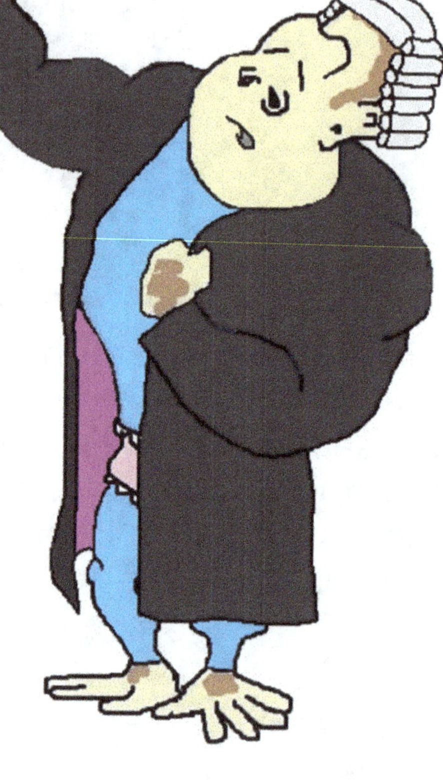

Magic E is also like a ninja!

He is silent!

But he can't just do it anytime he pleases!

He must be to the right of his friend,
and in this book at least, there must
be a letter between.

Let's get started...

Sounds

Vowels

Tracks 0-9

Track 5

	Name	Sound	
	A	a	
	E	e	
	I	i	
	O	o	
	U	u	

Long vowel sounds

Long vowels are easy! They're just the same as their names!

Track 6

But sometimes U cuts its name short.

Then its long sound is just "OO!"

Consonants

"Sometimes Sounds"

Many letters have "sometimes sounds."

Sometimes C sounds like S.

Sometimes G sounds like J.

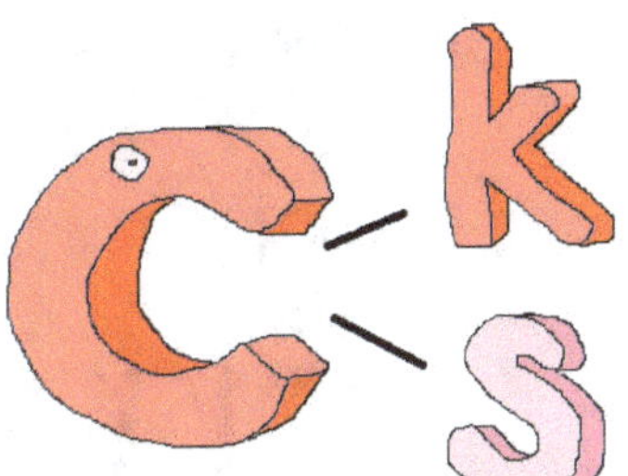

Magic E makes C and G say their sometimes sounds!

Listen, point, and make the sound:

Track 9 Words with  A

1  ak  ake ake

2  am  ame ame

3  at  ate ate

Listen, point, and say:

Track 10

1 cak + e = cake   cake

2 gam + e = game  game

3 lat + e = late   late

Follow the rules 

1 gat + e = ______ 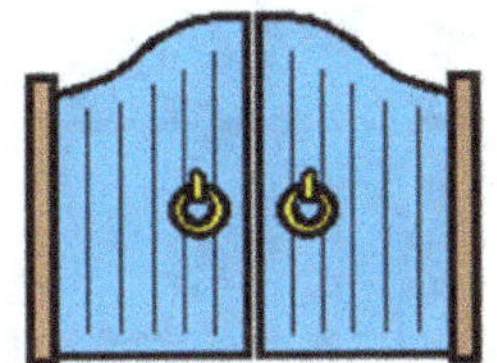

2 ap + e = ______ 

3 can + e = ______ 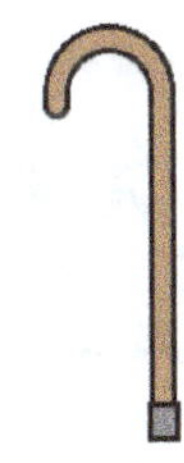

4 cav + e = ______ 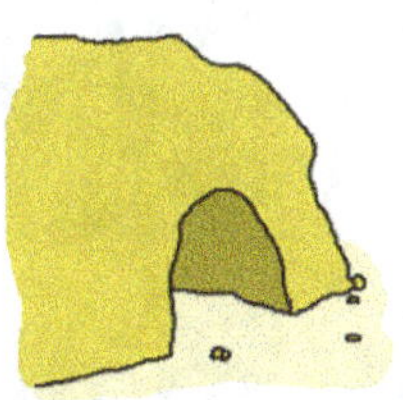

New Words

Listen, point and repeat the new words

Track
11

ake

bake   cake

ame

game   same

ane

cane   mane

ape

ape   cape

ate

gate   late

ave

cave   wave

Exercises

Track
12

Tracks 10-19

1  w v

2   c p

3  s m

4 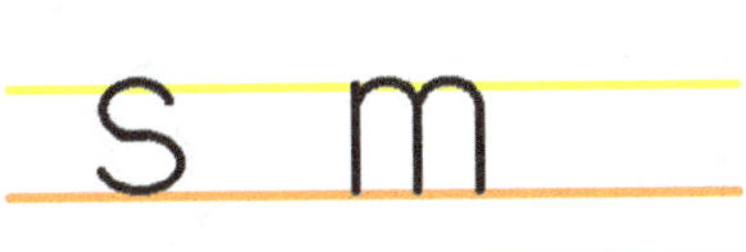 b k

Listen and circle the right letters AND picture

Track
13

1 ame ape ate 

2 ape ate ame 

3 ape ame ate 

4 ave ane ake 

5 ake ave ane 

6 ane ake ave 

Exercises

Circle the word you hear

Tracks 10-19

Track
14

Circle the last three letters of the word you hear

Track
15

1 ame ape ate   **2** ane ake ave

3 ame ape ate   **4** ane ake ave

Chant

Track
16

That ape has the same cane.

That ape has the same cape.

That ape has the same cane.

That ape has the same cape.

Story

Write the word to match the picture

Tracks 10-19

1. 

2. 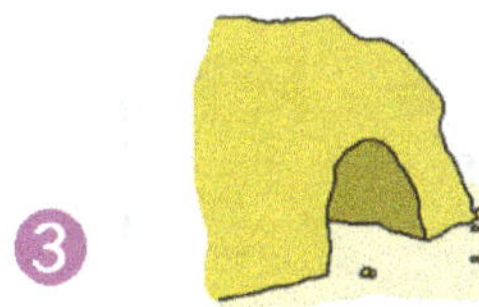

3. 

4. 

Listen and read along

Track 17

New sight words: don't   play

Review

Listen, point, and repeat all the words

Tracks 10-19

1

2

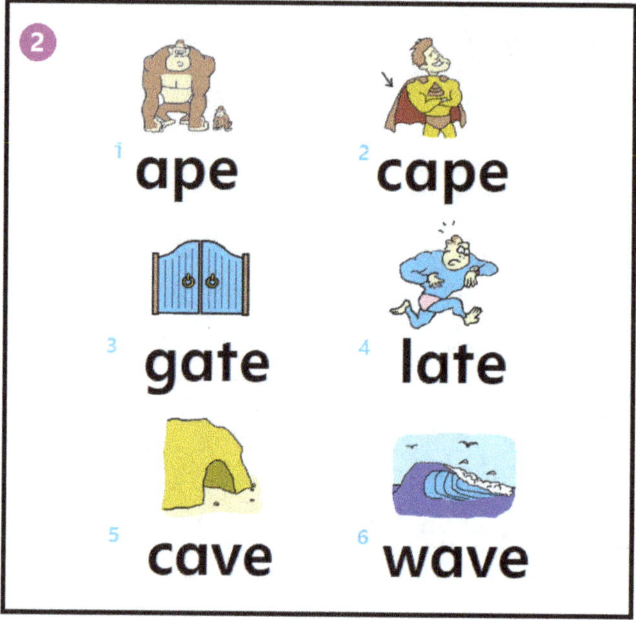

Listen to the final sound and circle the right picture

1     

2     

3     

4     

Review

1 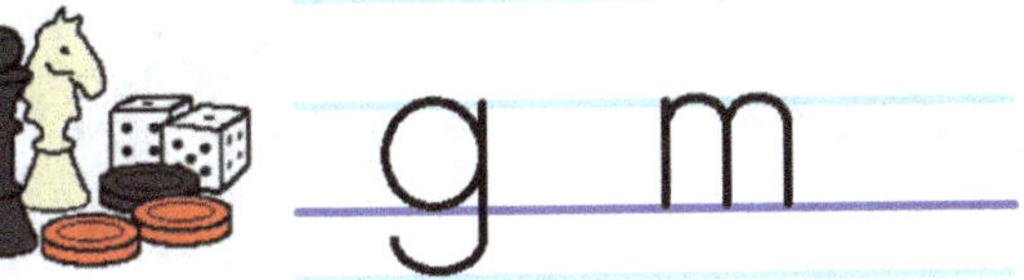 g __ m

2  __ __ p __

3  w __ v __

4  g __ t __

5  c __ k __

6  c __ n __

UNIT 2   Long Vowel Sounds

Listen, point, and make the sound:   Track 20   Words with **I**

Tracks 20-29

1    ik    ike

ike

2    it    ite

ite

3    iv    ive

ive

Listen, point, and say: Track 21

1   bik + e = bike      bike

2   kit + e = kite      kite

3   fiv + e = five   5   five

Follow the rules

Write the words

1   lin + e = __________ 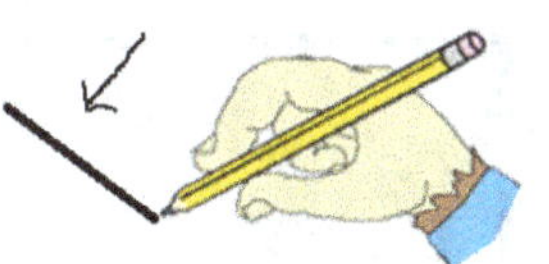

2   pip + e = __________ 

3   nin + e = __________ **9**

4   rid + e = __________ 

New Words

Listen, point and repeat the new words

ide

hide   **ride**

ike

bike   **hike**

ine

line   **nine**

ipe

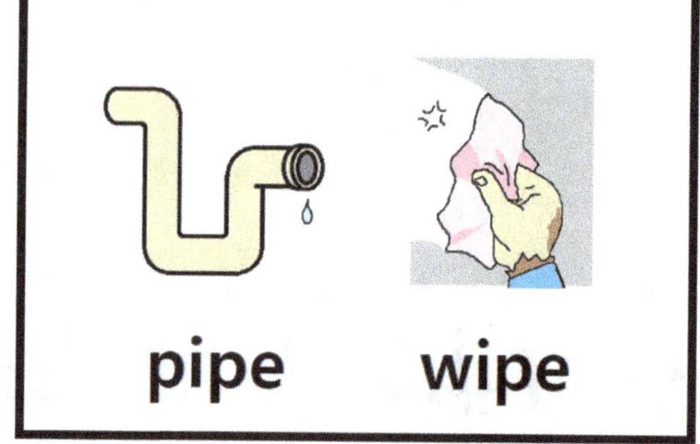

pipe   **wipe**

ite

bite   **kite**

ive

five   **hive**

Exercises

Listen and write the missing letters

Tracks 20-29

1 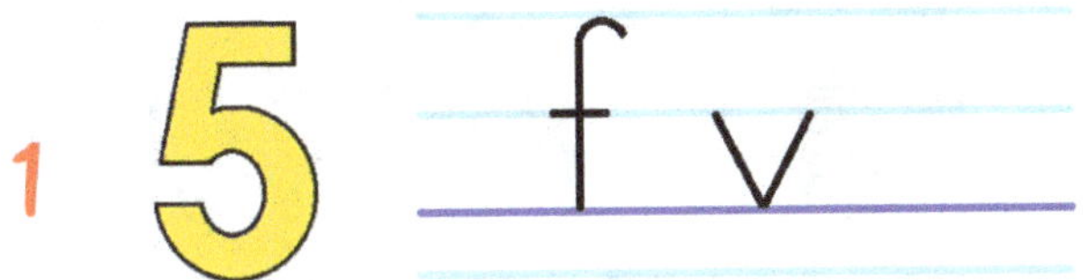 f v

2  h k

3 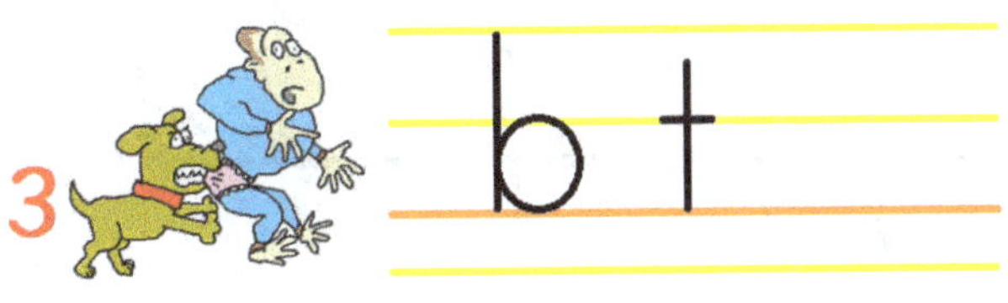 b t

4 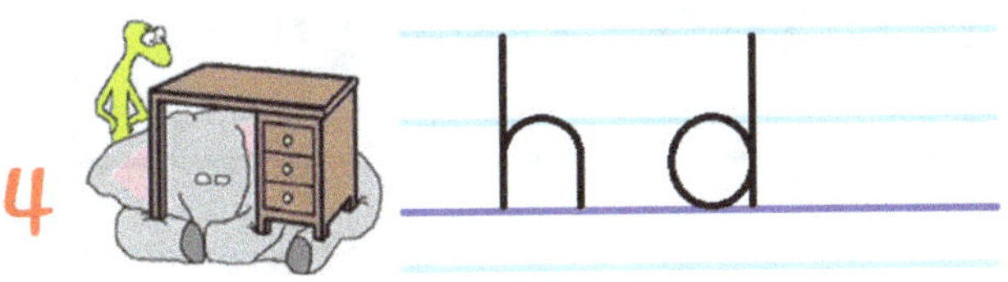 h d

Listen and circle the right letters AND picture

1 ide   ike   ine   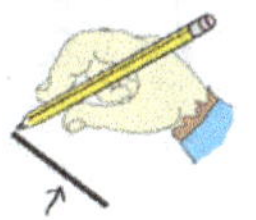

2 ide   ike   ine   

3 ide   ike   ine   

4 ipe   ite   ive   

5 ipe   ite   ive   

6 ipe   ite   ive   

Exercises

Circle the word you hear

Tracks 20-29 · Track 25

Circle the last three letters of the word you hear · Track 26

1. **ide** **ike** **ine**   2. **ipe** **ite** **ive**

3. **ide** **ike** **ine**   4. **ipe** **ite** **ive**

Chant · Track 27   New sight words: at   but   after

I like to hike and ride a bike.

Nine to five I'm at the hive,

But after five I like to hike.

I like to hike and ride a bike.

Story

Write the word to match the picture

 Tracks 20-29

 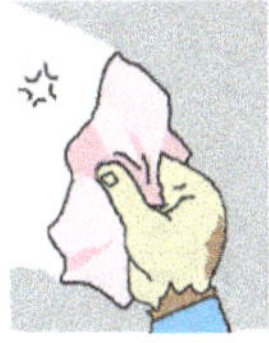 **1**

  **2**

3

4

Listen and read along

Track 28

New sight words: fly

Review

Listen, point, and repeat all the words

Tracks 20-29

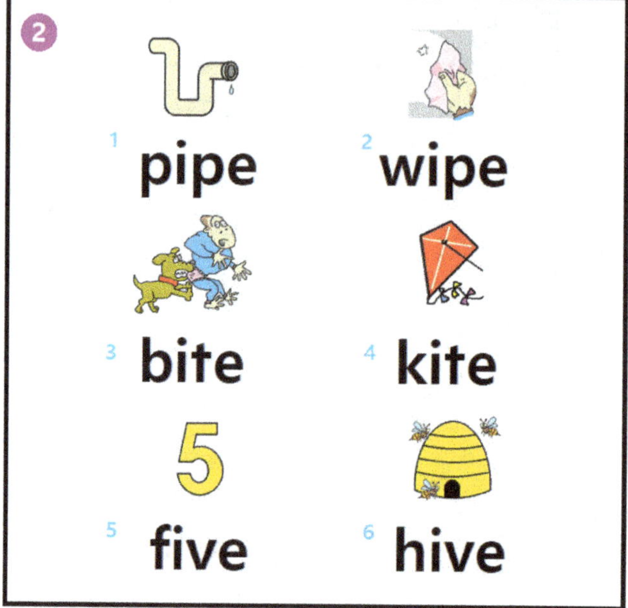

Listen to the final sound and circle the right picture

1        2     

3        4   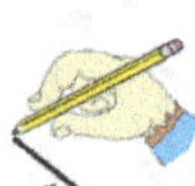  

Say the word and write it

1  g

2 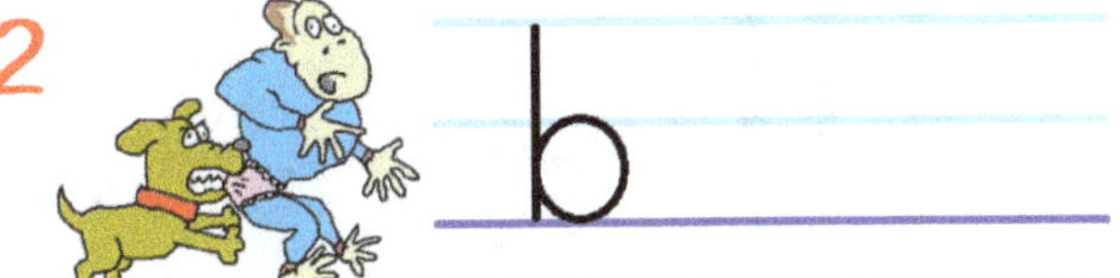 b

3 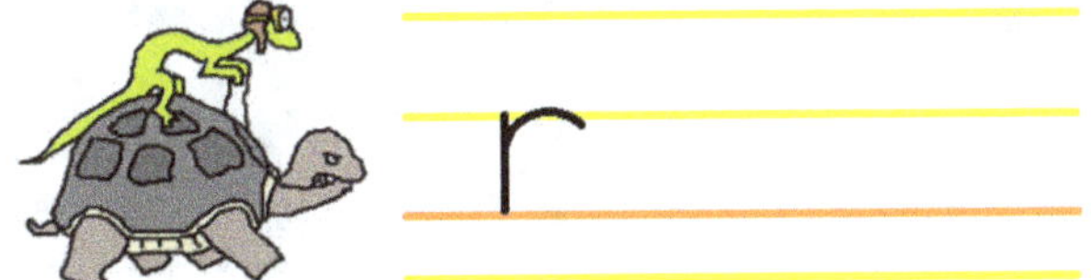 r

4 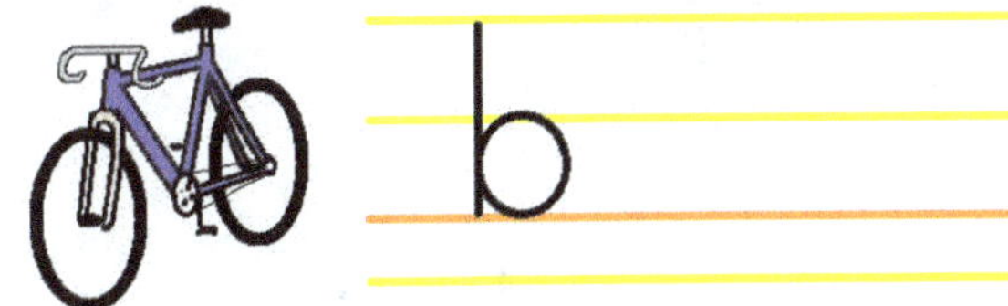 b

5  c

6 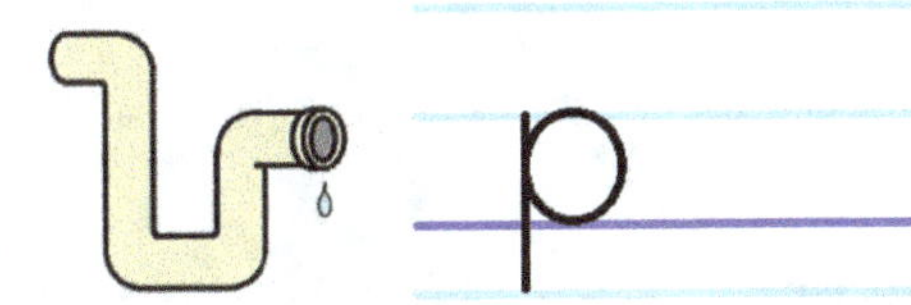 p

UNIT 3   Long Vowel Sounds

Listen, point, and make the sound:   Track 31   Words with  O

1    ol    ole   ole

2    on    one   one

(Not to be confused with the number 1)

3    op    ope   ope

Listen, point, and say: Track 32

1   mol + e = mole      mole

2   bon + e = bone   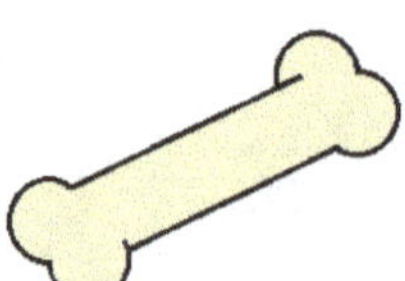   bone

3   rop + e = rope      rope

Follow the rules 

Write the words

1 jok + e = __________ 

2 not + e = __________ 

3 glob + e = __________ 

4 pok + e = __________ 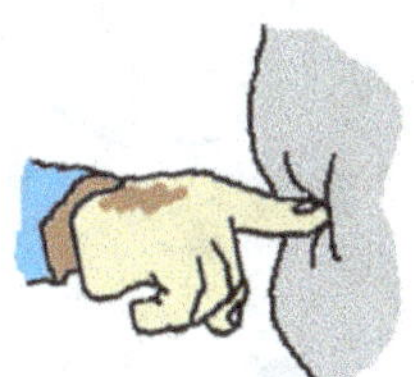

New Words

Listen, point and repeat the new words

Tracks 30-39

obe

globe   robe

oke

joke   poke

ole

hole   mole

one

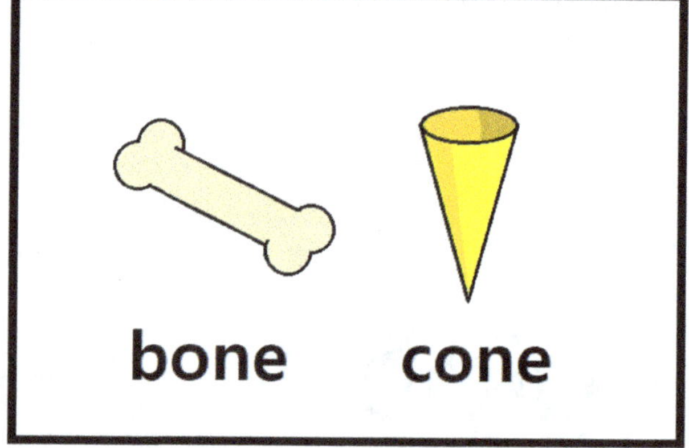

bone   cone

ope

hope   rope

ote

note   vote

Exercises

Listen and write the missing letters

Tracks 30-39

1 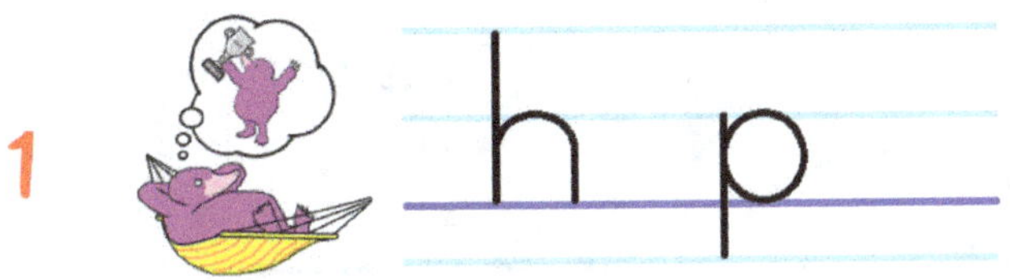 h p   2 c n

3 h l   4 v t

Listen and circle the right letters AND picture

1 obe oke ole    2 oke obe ole 

3 obe oke ole    4 one ope ote 

5 one ote ope    6 one ope ote 

Exercises

Circle the word you hear

Tracks 30-39

Track 36

Circle the last three letters of the word you hear

Track 37

1. obe   oke   ole   2. one   ope   ote

3. obe   oke   ole   4. one   ope   ote

Chant

Track 38

New sight words: for   best

Vote for mole! Vote for mole!
He's the best mole in the hole

Vote for mole! Vote for mole!
He's the best mole in the hole

Story

Write the word to match the picture

Tracks 30-39

1

2

3

4

Listen and read along

Track 39

New words: make   ice cream

Review

Listen, point, and repeat all the words

Tracks 40-49

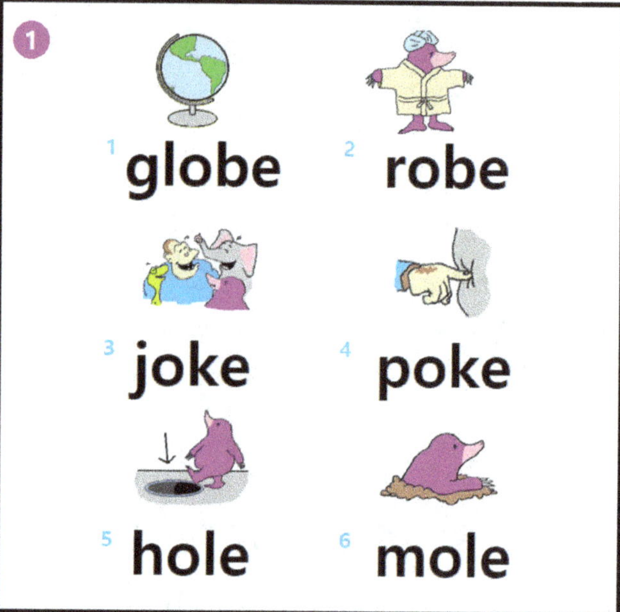

1. globe
2. robe
3. joke
4. poke
5. hole
6. mole

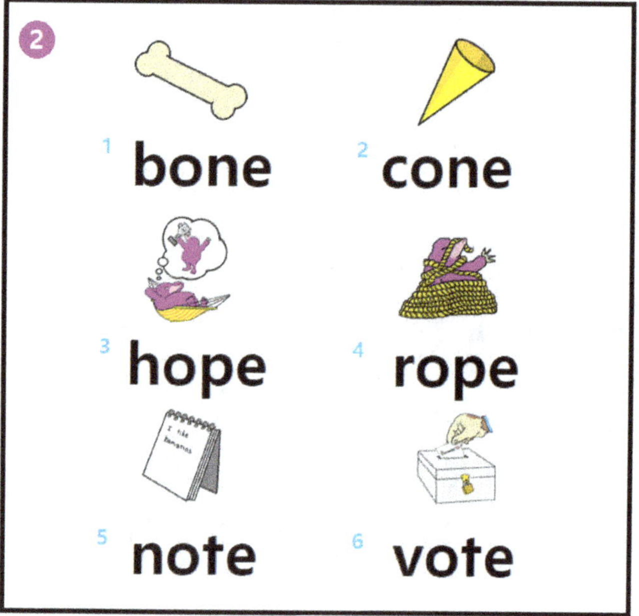

1. bone
2. cone
3. hope
4. rope
5. note
6. vote

Listen to the final sound and circle the right picture

1   

2   

3 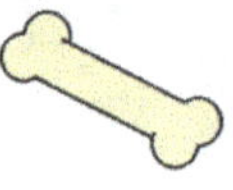  5

4   

Review

1 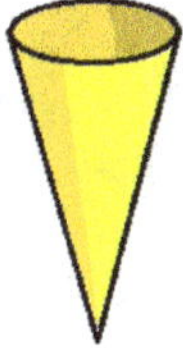

2 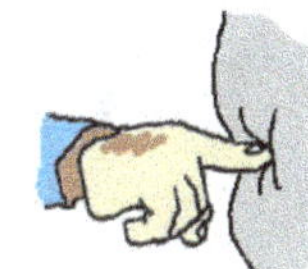

3 

4 

5 

6 

Listen, point, and make the sound:   Track 42   Words with U

Tracks 40-49

1 ub    ube   ube

2 un    une   une

3 ut    ute   ute

Listen, point, and say: Track 43

1 cub + e = cube   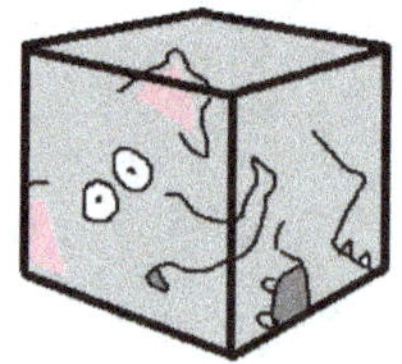 cube

2 dun + e = dune    dune

3 cut + e = cute    cute

Follow the rules

Write the words

1 mul + e = __________ 

2 fus + e = __________ 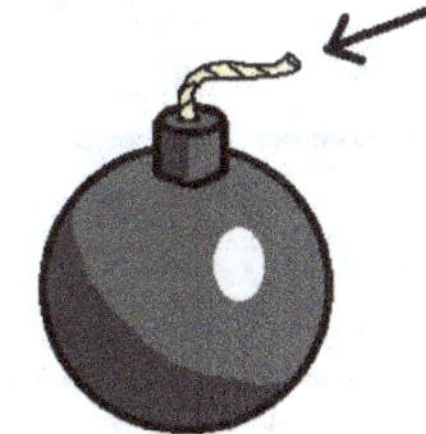

3 pur + e = __________ 

4 us + e = __________ 

New Words

Listen, point and repeat the new words

Track 44

ube

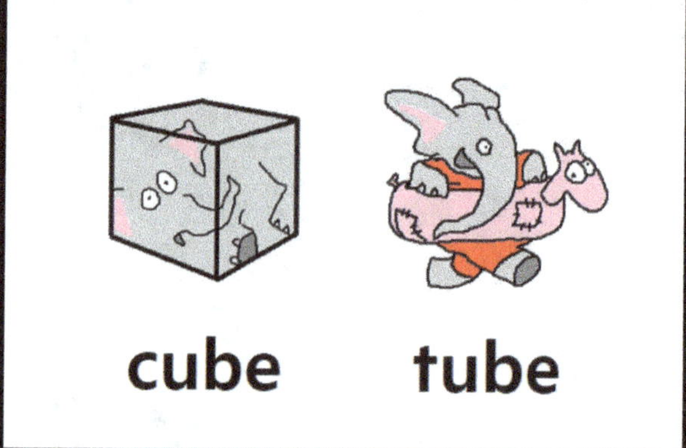

cube   tube

ule

mule   rule

une

dune   tune

ure

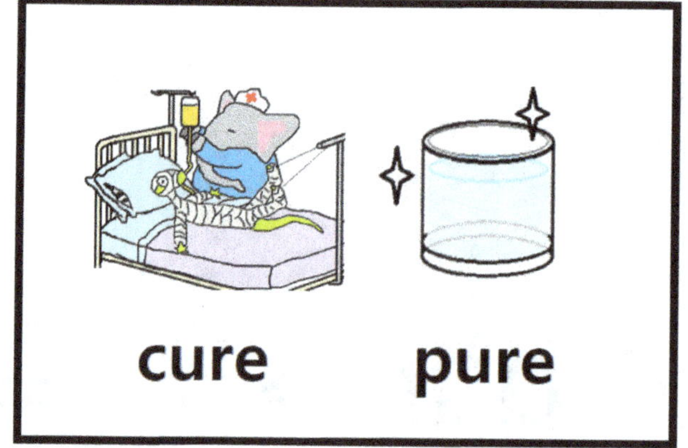

cure   pure

use

fuse   use

ute

cute   mute

Exercises

Listen and write the missing letters

1  t _ b

2  r _ l

3  t _ n

4  m _ t

Listen and circle the right letters AND picture

1 ube ule une 

2 ube une ule 

3 ube ule une 

4 ure use ute 

5 use ure ute 

6 ure use ute 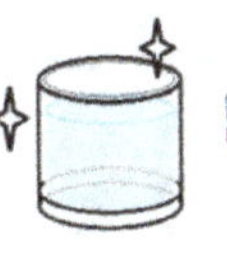

Exercises

Circle the word you hear

Circle the last three letters of the word you hear

1 ube   ule   une   2 ure   use   ute

3 ube   ule   une   4 ure   use   ute

Chant

Cute mule play a tune!
Cute mule play a tune!
Cute mule play a tune!
Play a tune, cute mule!

Story

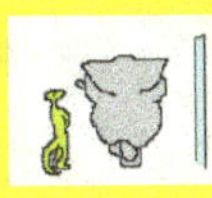

Write the word to match the picture

1. 

2. 

3. 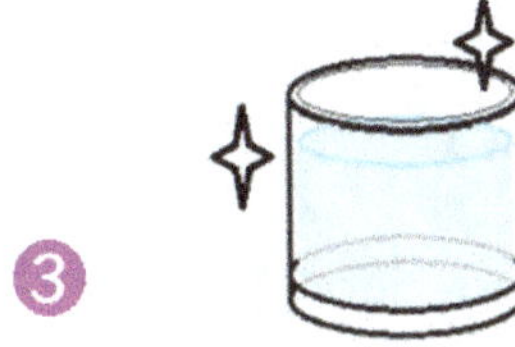

4. 

Listen and read along

New sight words: doctor   is

Review

Listen, point, and repeat all the words

Tracks 50-59

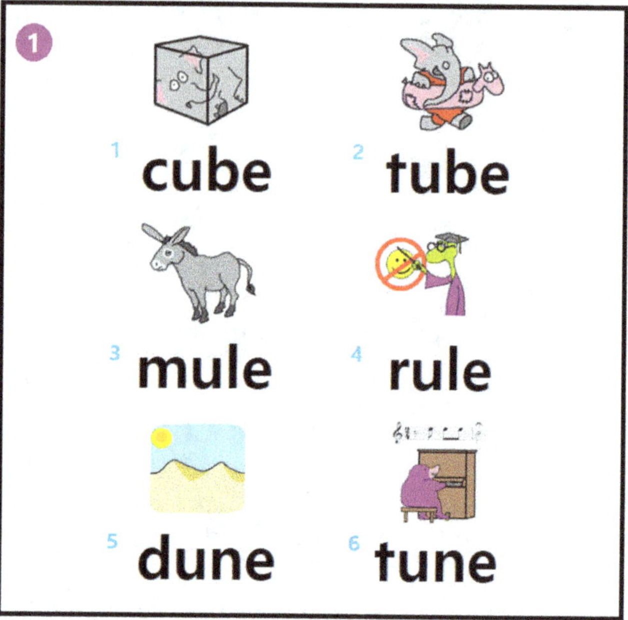

Listen to the final sound and circle the right picture

1   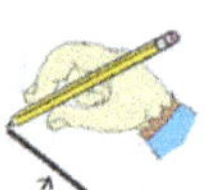   2   

3      4   

Review  

Say the word and write it

1 

2 

3 

4

5 

6 

UNIT 5　Long Vowel Sounds

Listen, point, and make the sound:  **Words with A, I, O, U**

Tracks 50-59

Track 53

1　ad　　ade

2　ac　　ace

3　ir　　ire

Listen, point, and say:

Track 54

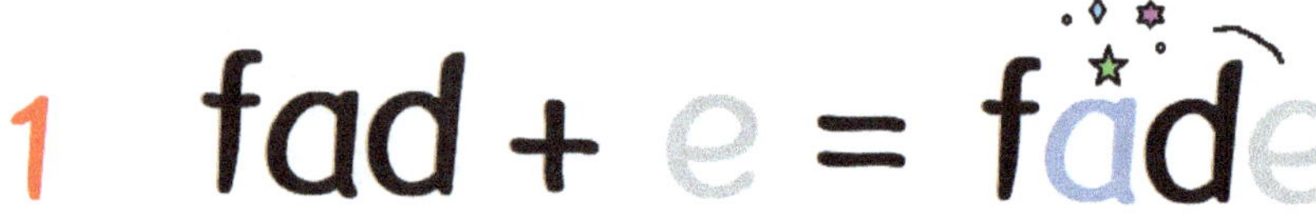

1　fad + e = fade　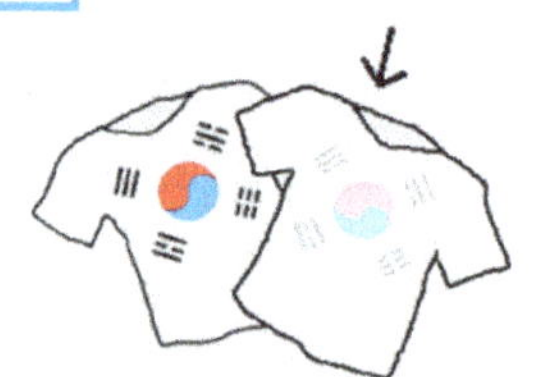　fade

2　fac + e = face　　face

3　tir + e = tire　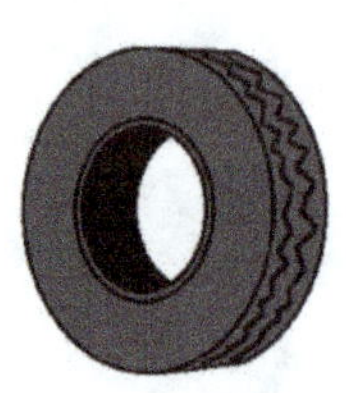　tire

Follow the rules 

Write the words

1 sor + e = __________ 

2 duk + e = __________ 

3 mad + e = __________ 

4 nic + e = __________ 

New Words

Listen, point and repeat the new words

ade

fade   made

ire

fire   tire

ore

more   sore

uke

duke   uke

ace / ice

face   nice

Exercises

Listen and write the missing letters

Tracks 50-59

1 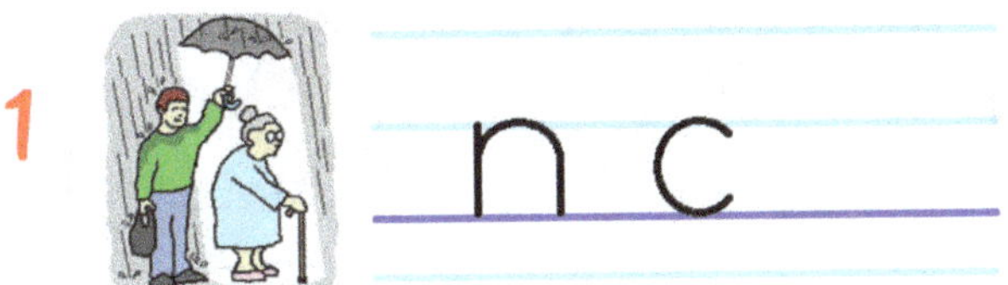 n c

2 m d

3 m r

4 k

Listen and circle the right letters AND picture

1 uke ire ore 

2 ade ice ore 

3 uke ore ace 

4 ade ice ire 

5 ire ade ore 

6 ore ire ade 

Exercises

Circle the word you hear

Tracks 50-59

Circle the last three letters of the word you hear

1. ade   ire   uke
2. ore   ace   ire
3. ace   ire   ade
4. ore   uke   ice

Chant

New sight words: him   people   yell

Duke Duke played the uke
It made him very sore
Duke Duke played the uke
The people yelled
"MORE, MORE!"

Write the word to match the picture

Tracks 60-69

1.

2.

3.

4.

Listen and read along

Track 61

Review

Listen, point, and repeat all the words

Track 62

Tracks 60-69

1
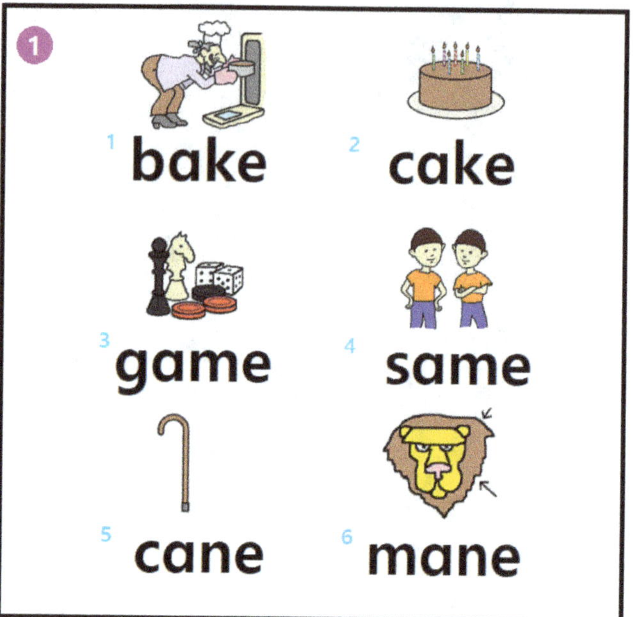

1 bake 2 cake
3 game 4 same
5 cane 6 mane

2

1 ape 2 cape
3 gate 4 late
5 cave 6 wave

3
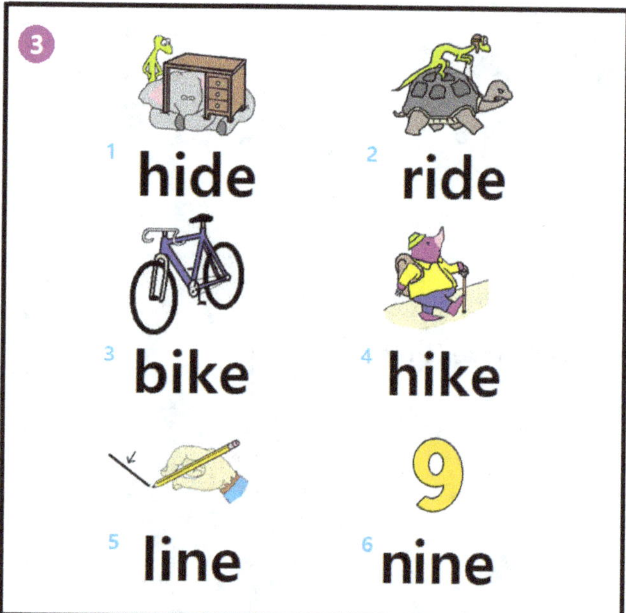

1 hide 2 ride
3 bike 4 hike
5 line 6 nine

4

1 pipe 2 wipe
3 bite 4 kite
5 five 6 hive

Review

Track 63

Tracks 60-69

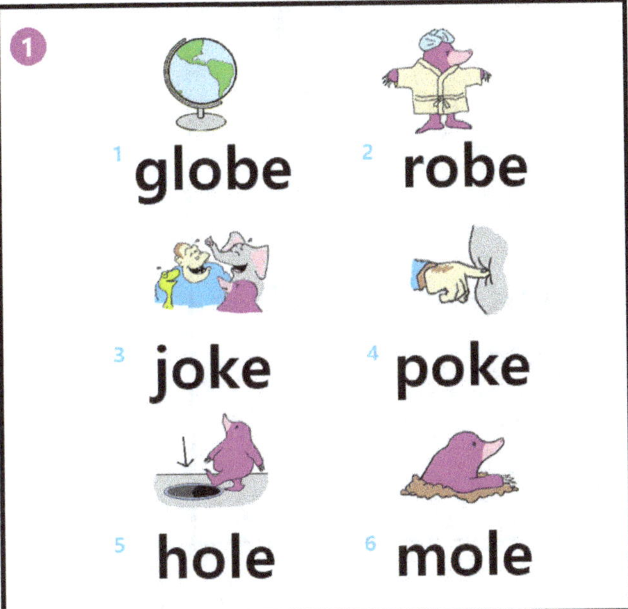

1
1. globe
2. robe
3. joke
4. poke
5. hole
6. mole

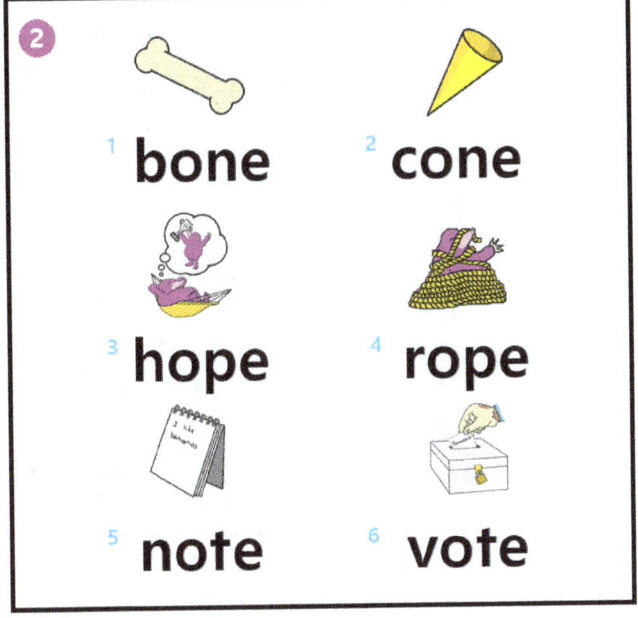

2
1. bone
2. cone
3. hope
4. rope
5. note
6. vote

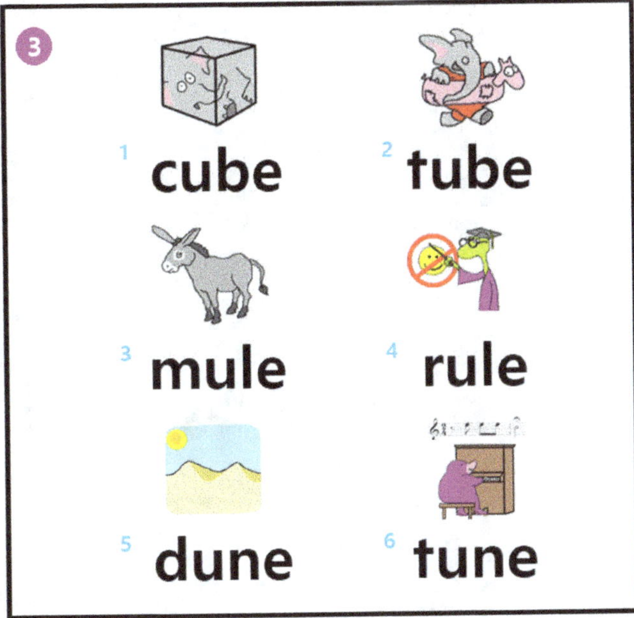

3
1. cube
2. tube
3. mule
4. rule
5. dune
6. tune

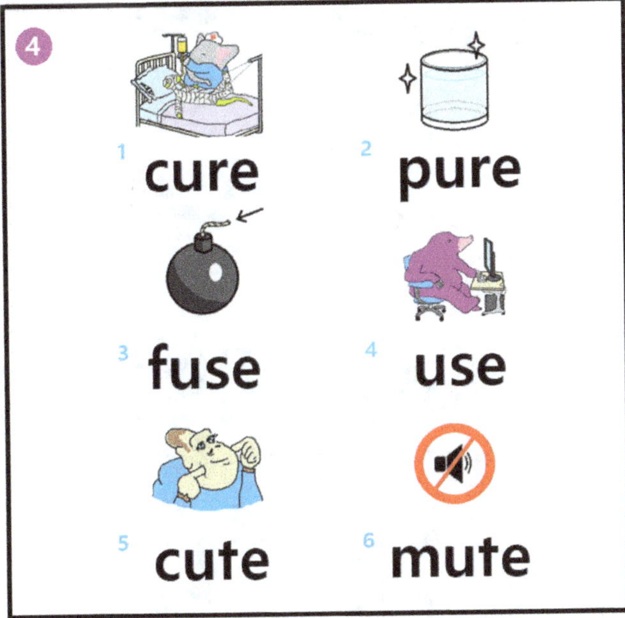

4
1. cure
2. pure
3. fuse
4. use
5. cute
6. mute

Review

Listen, point, and repeat all the words  

Track 64

Tracks 60-69

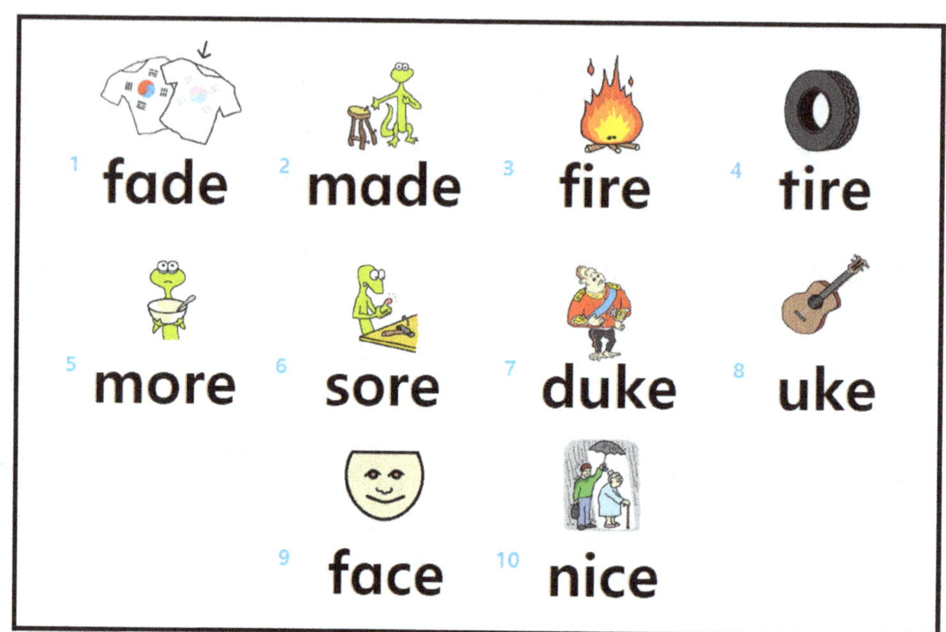

Find the path

A
I
O
U

9

a
i
o
u

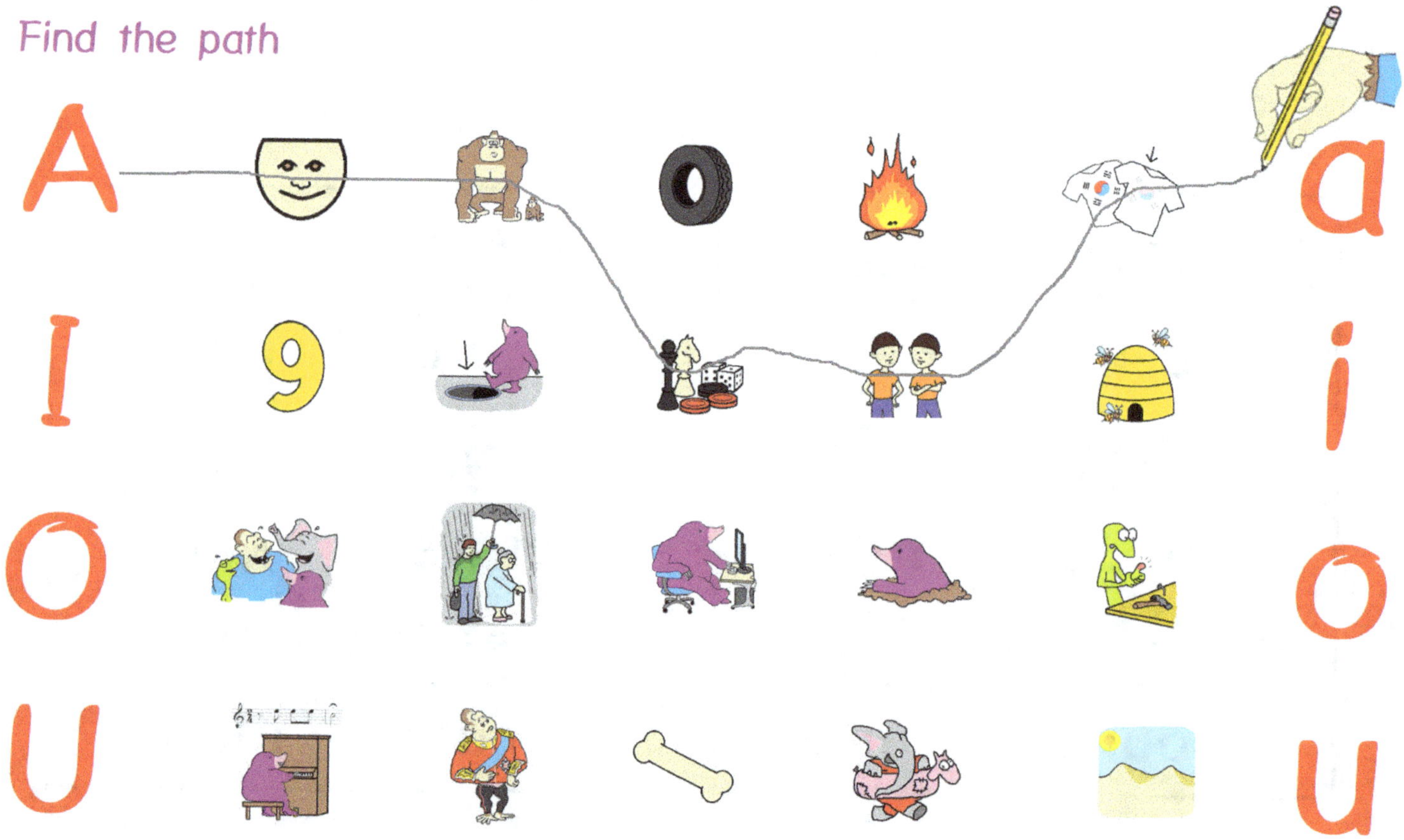

Review

1 

2 

3 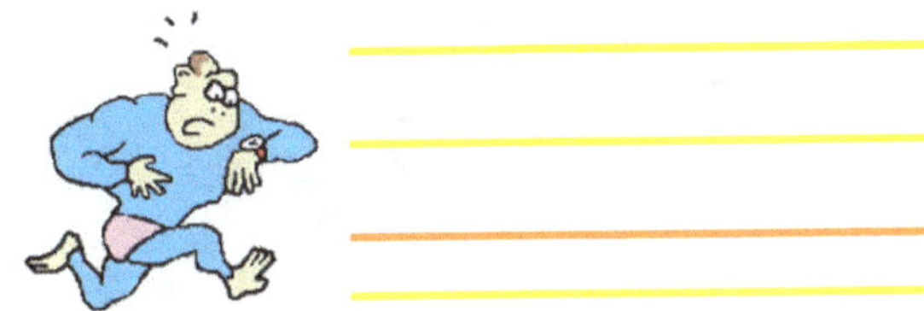

4 

5 

6 

Listen and circle the word you hear

a  b  c 

Tracks 70-79

1      

2      

3      

4  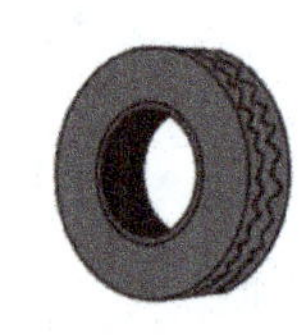    

5      

Test

Listen and write the long sound a 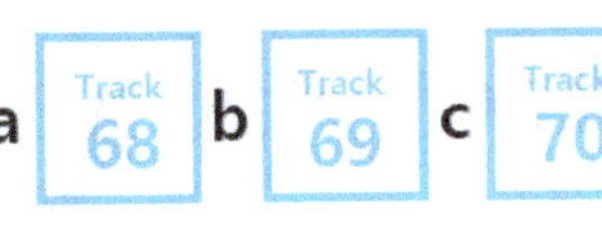 b c 

Tracks 60-69

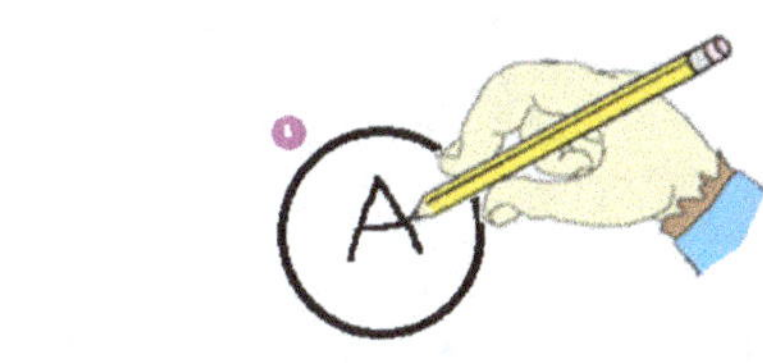

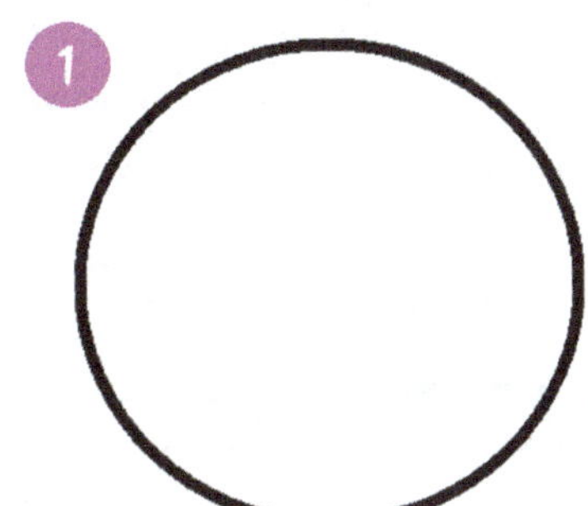

1

2

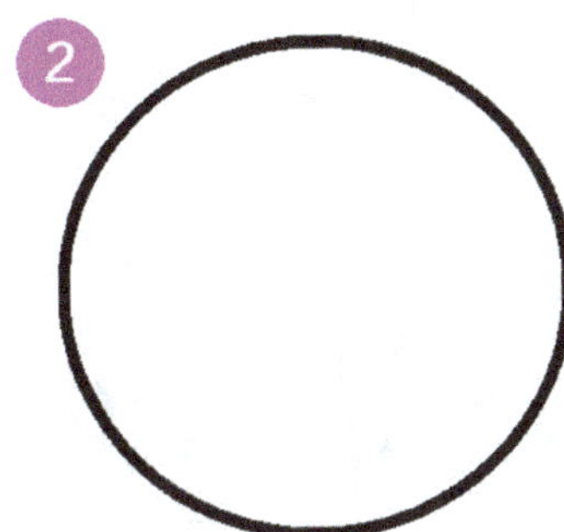

3

4

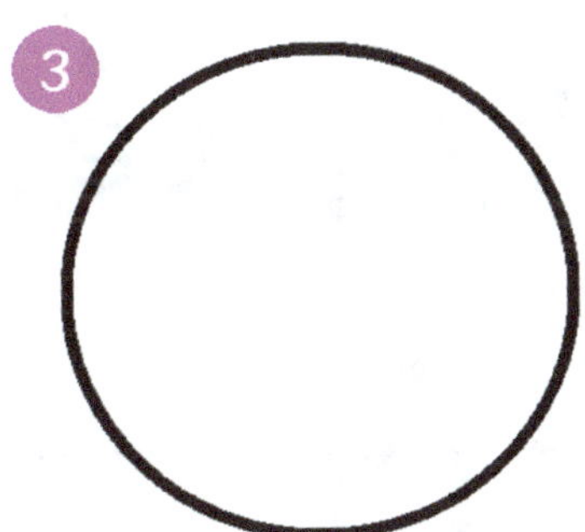

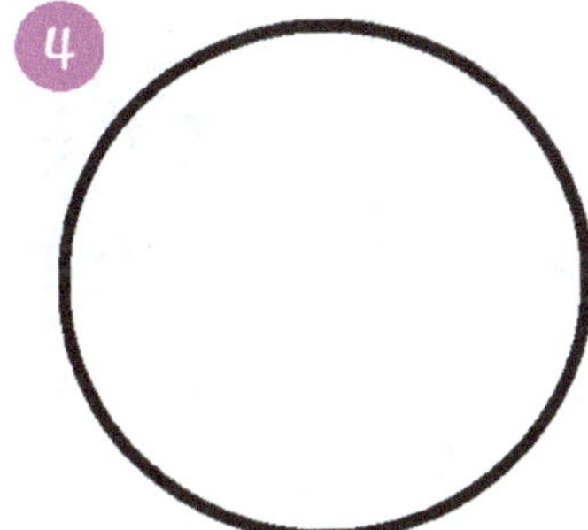

5

6

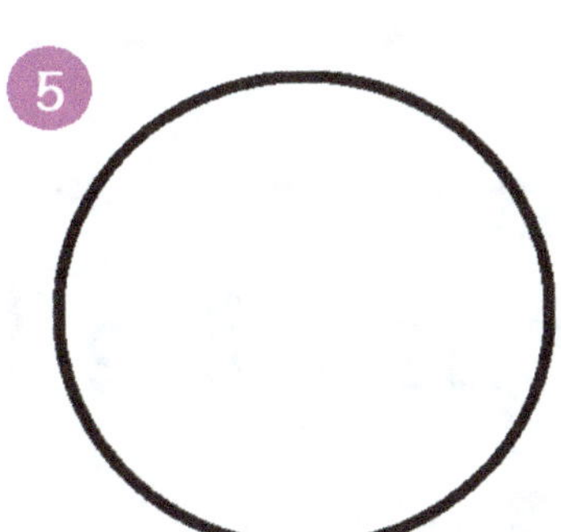

Test

Listen and circle the last three letters a [71] b [72] c [73]

Tracks 70-74

1  | uke | ame | ole | ide

2  | ate | one | use | ire

3  | ote | ake | ipe | ube

4  | ave | ine | ute | oke

5 | ape | ule | ope | ike

Look, listen and write the word

Track
74

Tracks 70-74

1 

2 

3 

4 

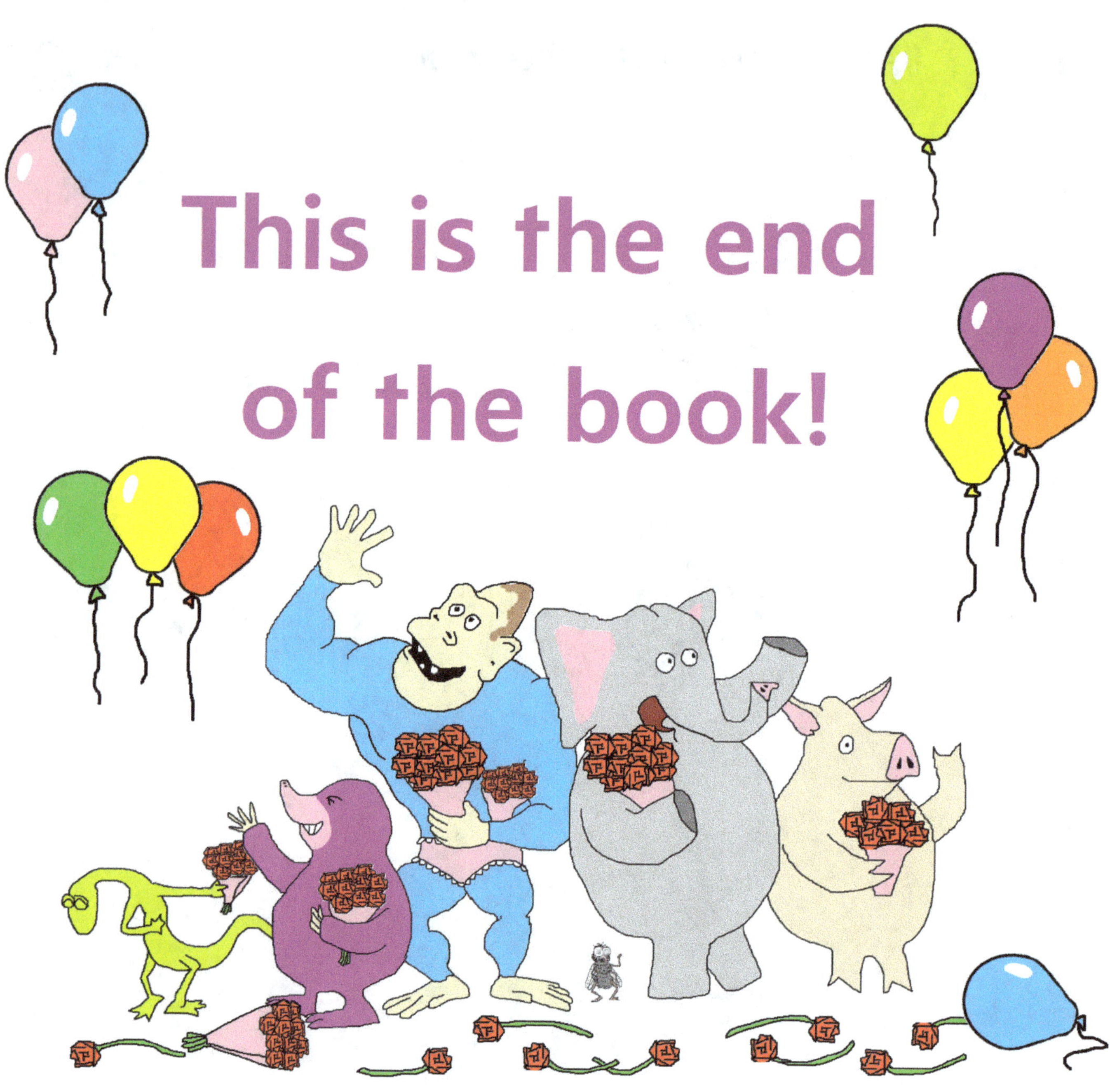
This is the end
of the book!

Word List

Unit 1

 cake    bake    game    same

 cane    mane    ape   cape

 gate    late    cave    wave

Unit 2

 hide    ride    bike    hike

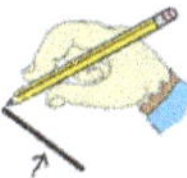 line    nine    pipe    wipe

 bite    kite    five    hive

Unit 3

  globe    robe    joke    poke

 hole    mole   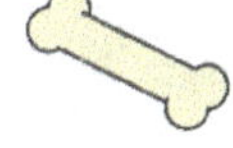 bone    cone

 hope    rope    note    vote

Word List

Unit 4

 cube    tube    mule    rule

 dune    tune    cure    pure

 fuse    use    cute    mute

Unit 5

 fade    made    fire    tire

 more    sore    duke    uke

 face    nice

OUR SIGHT WORD FLASH CARDS!

don't	play
at	but
after	fly

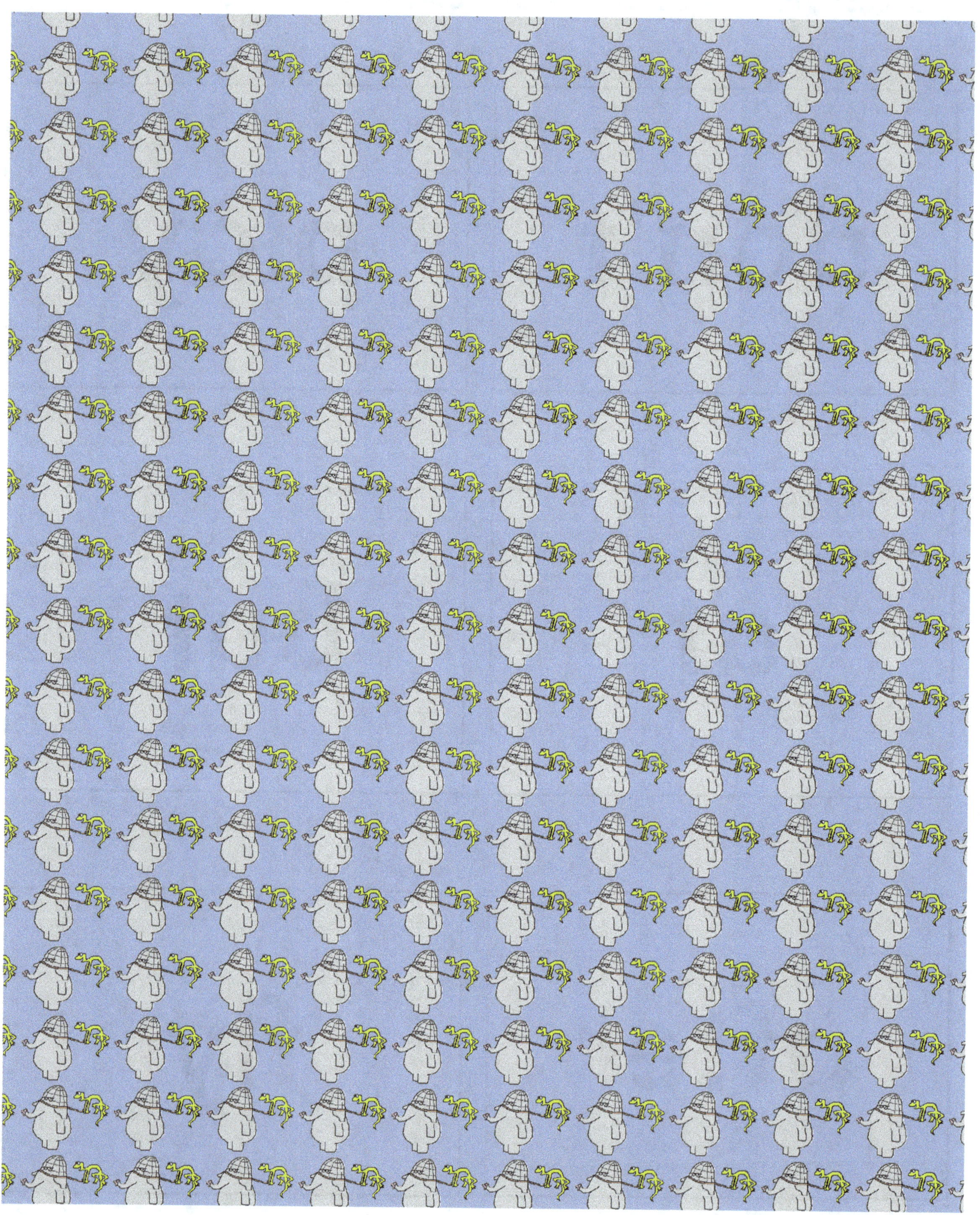

OUR SIGHT WORD FLASH CARDS!

for

best

make

doctor

is

him

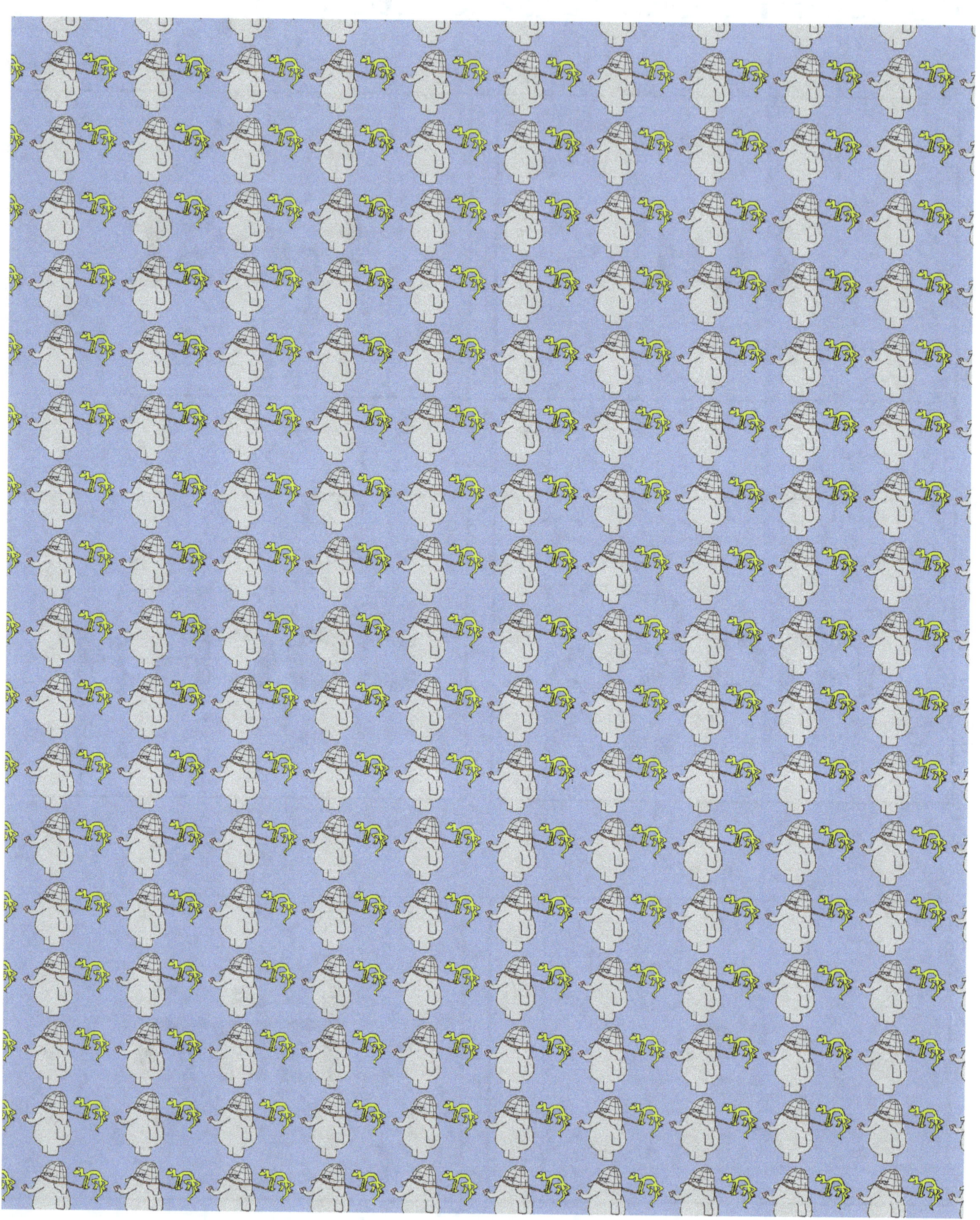

OUR SIGHT WORD FLASH CARDS! 

people

yell

my

am

she

wear

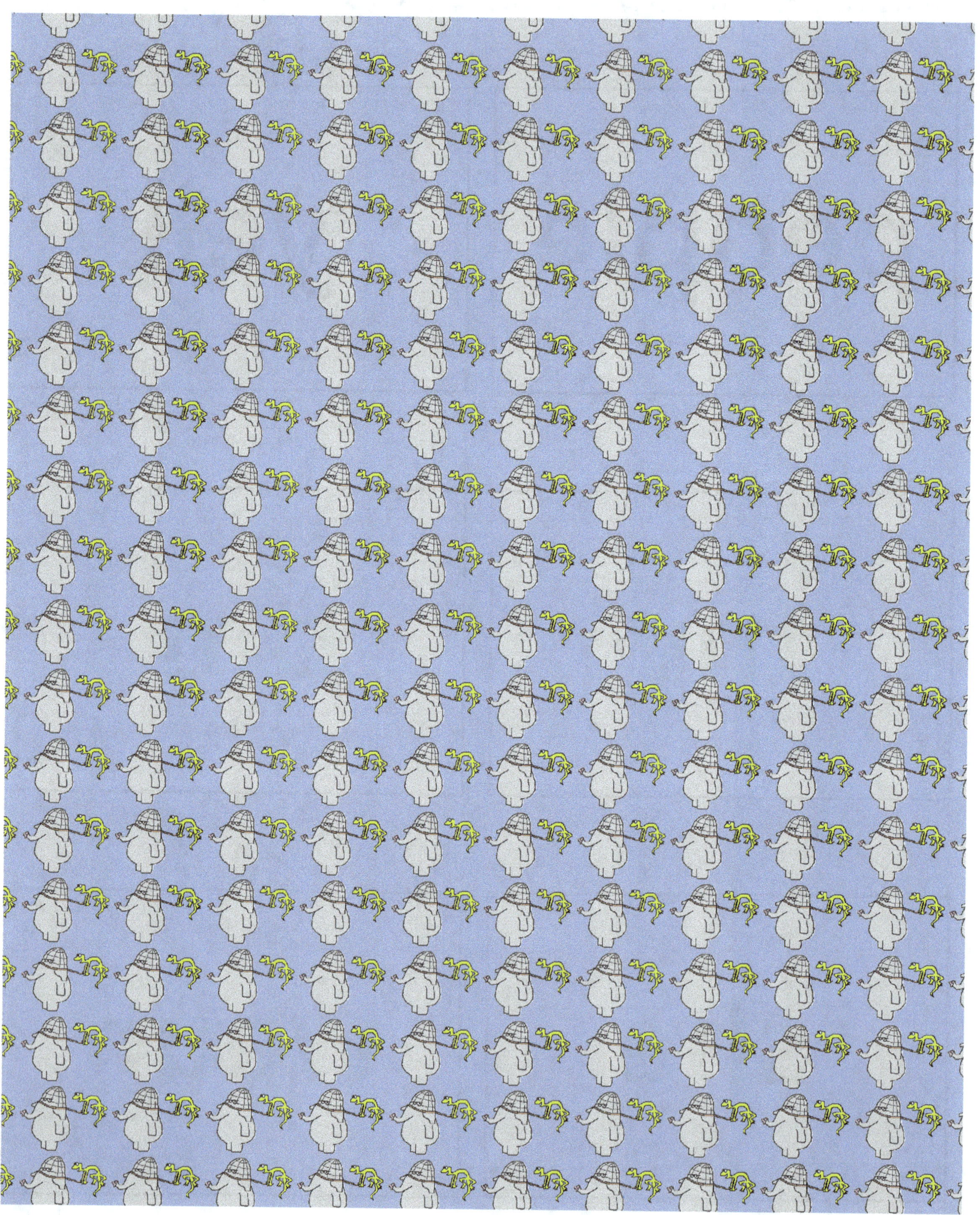

OUR SIGHT WORD FLASH CARDS!

so	will
want	give
me	have

OUR SIGHT WORD FLASH CARDS! 

he

handsome

pretty

let's

what

cent

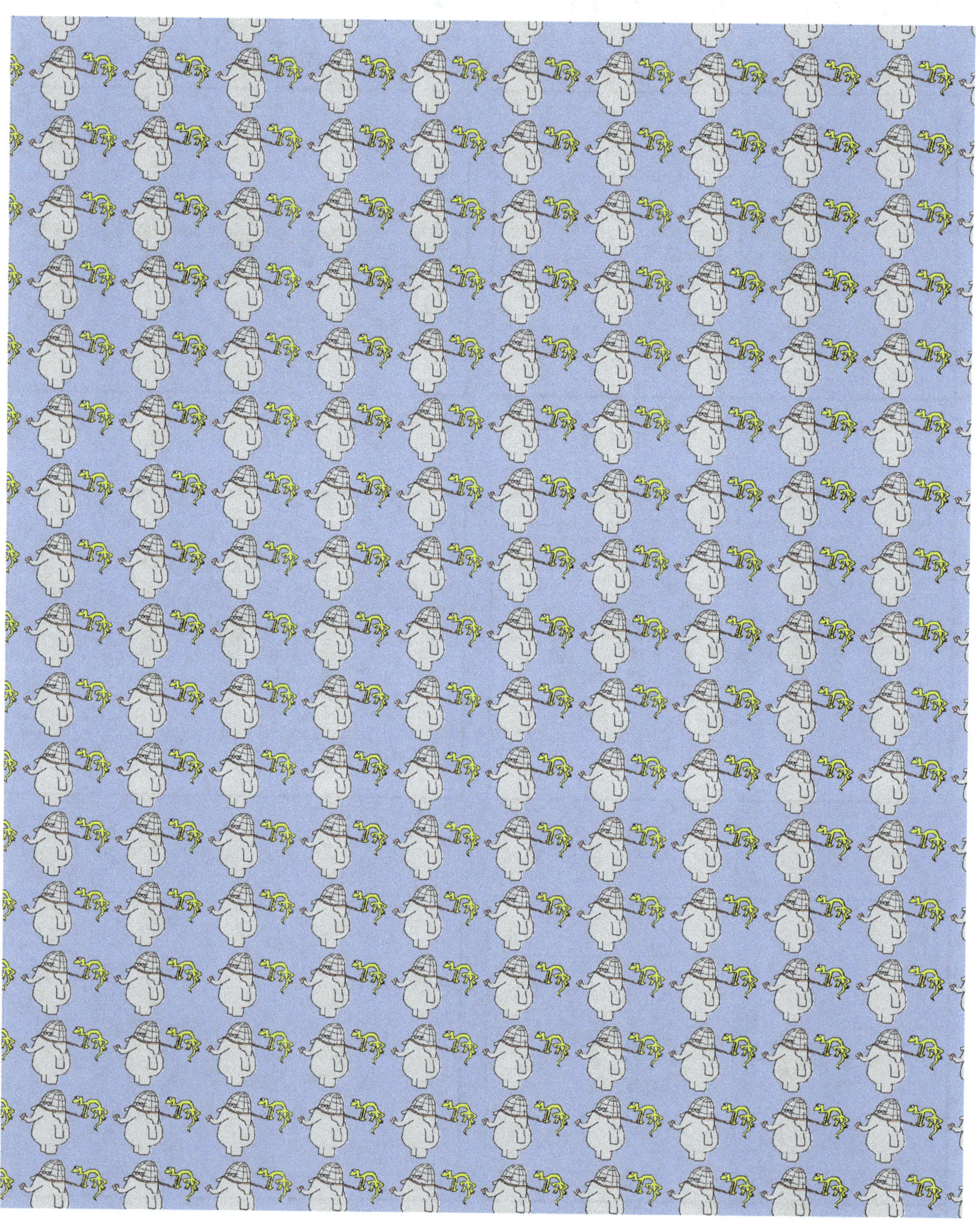

OUR SIGHT WORD FLASH CARDS!

see	call
must	need
a / an	and

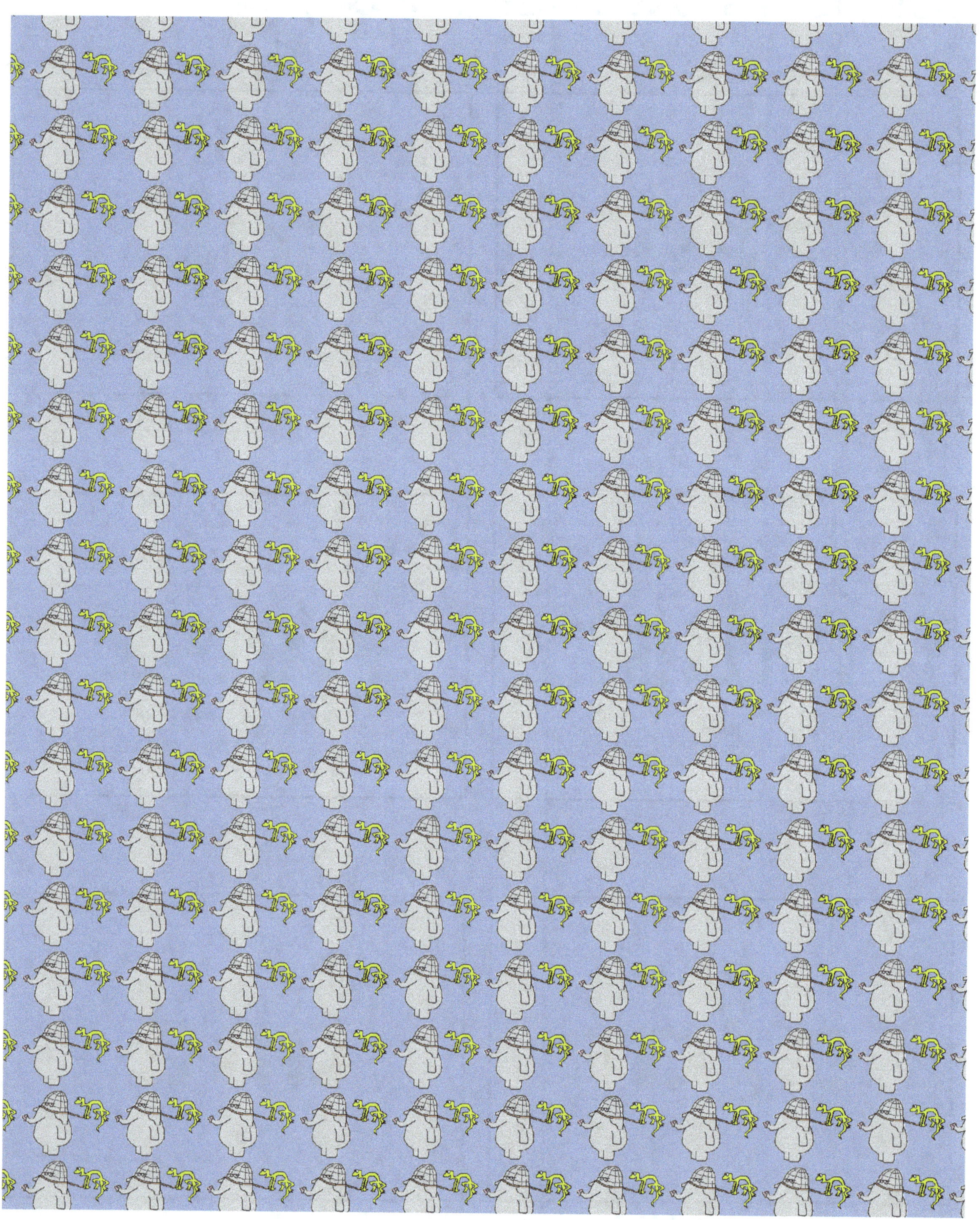

all

on

in

the

no

lift

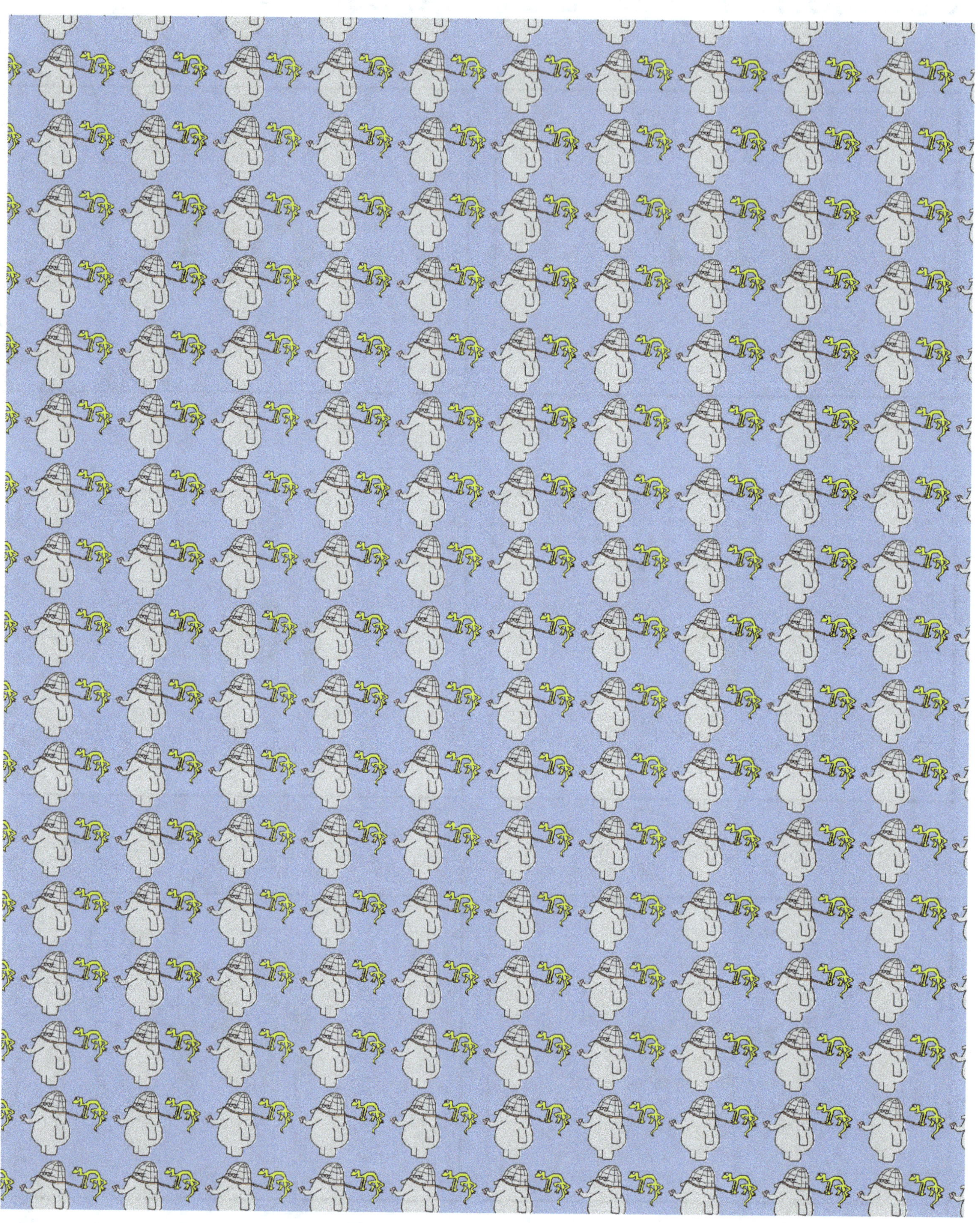

OUR SIGHT WORD FLASH CARDS!

like

get

oh

not

did

you

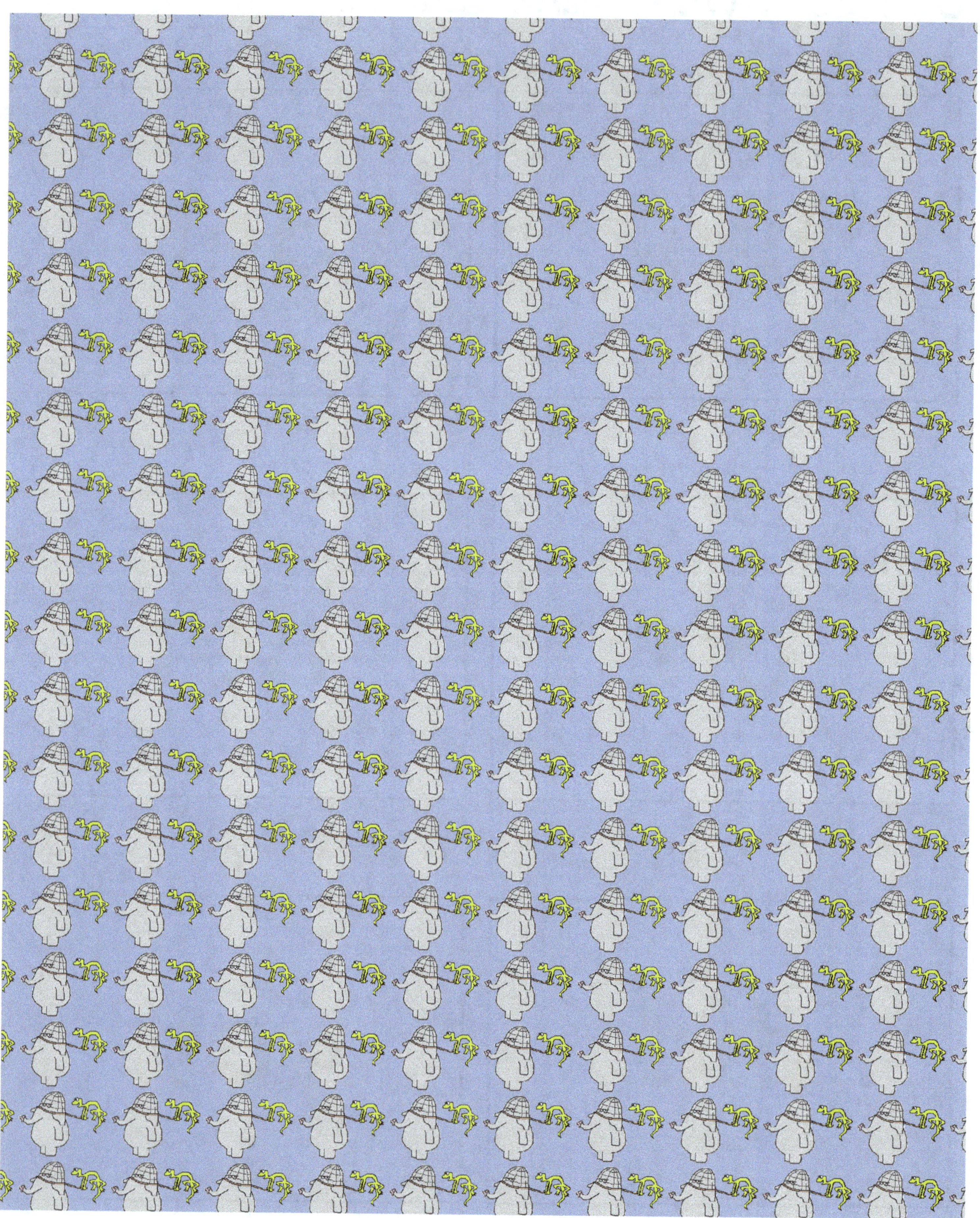

OUR SIGHT WORD FLASH CARDS!

your

has

put

one

by

say

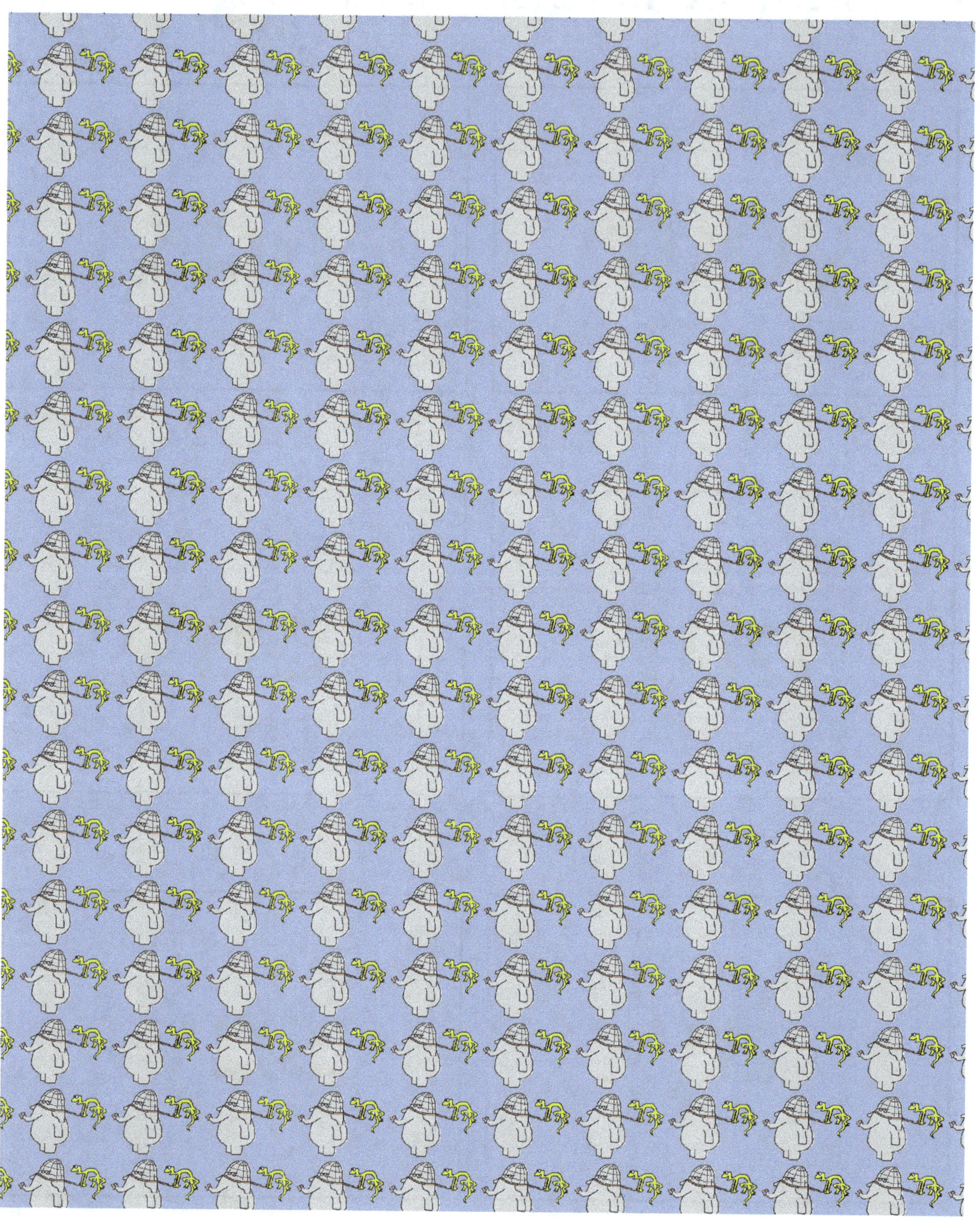

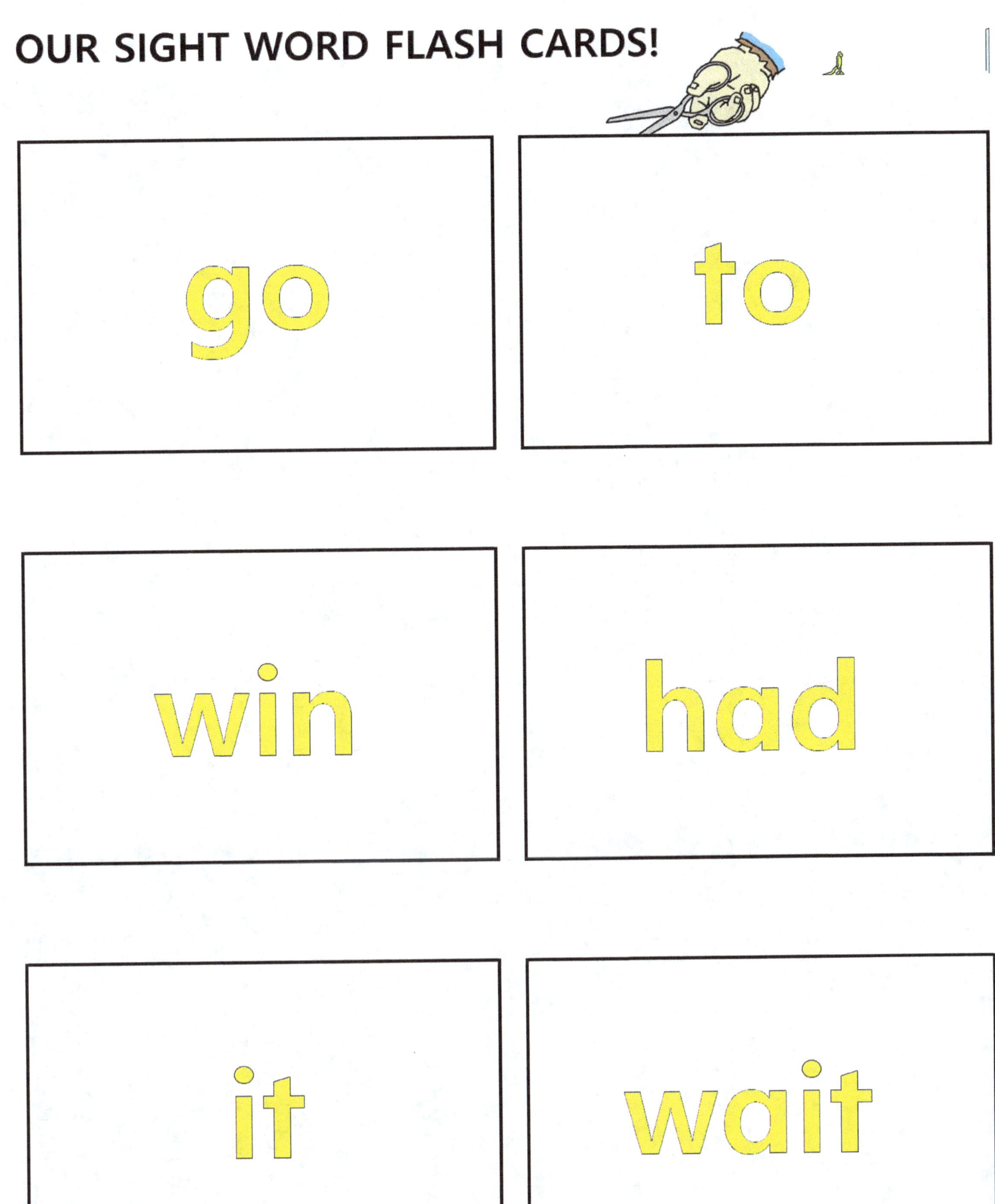

go
to
win
had
it
wait

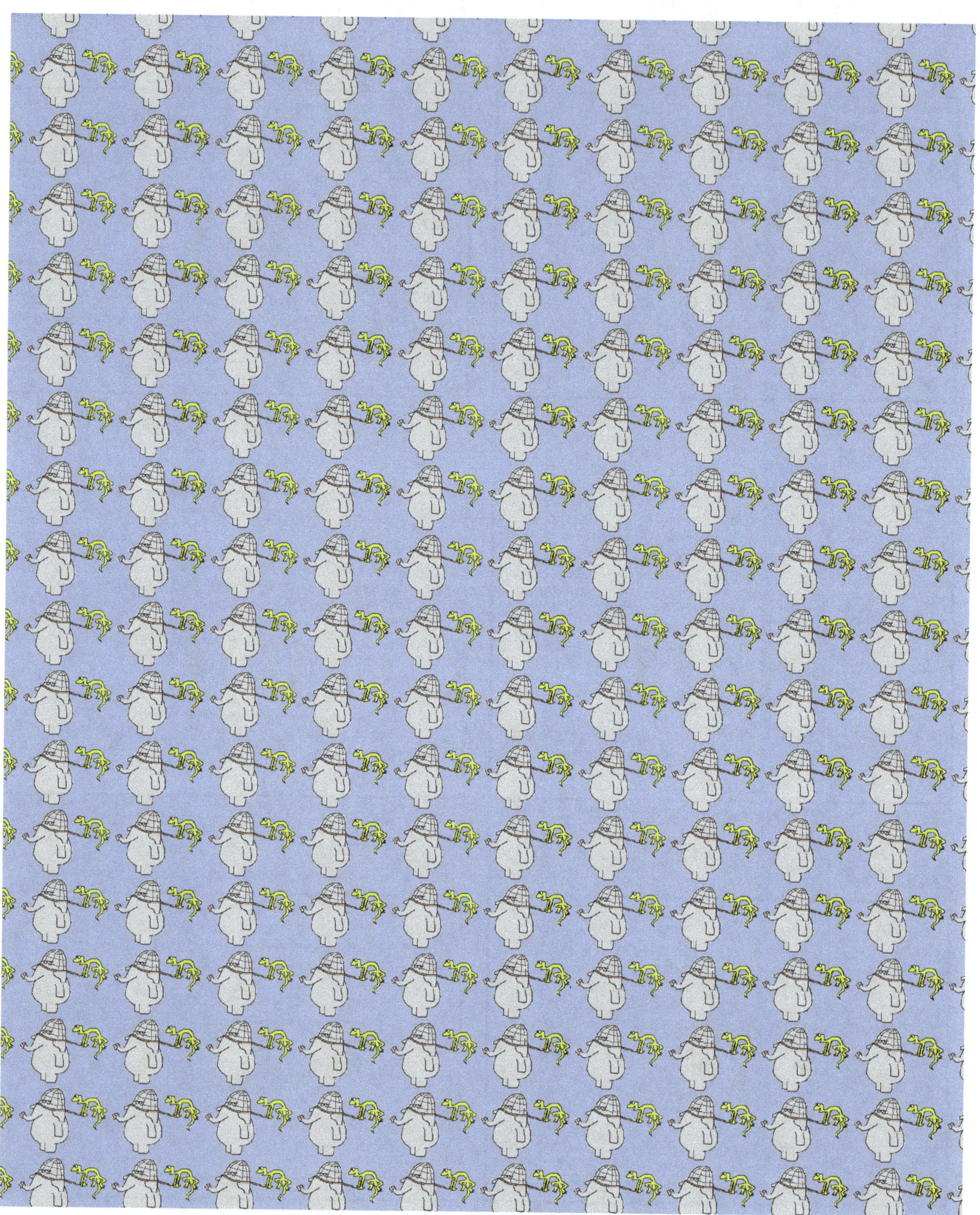

Coloring Pages!!

A

CAPE

Coloring Pages!!

I

BITE

O

JOKE

Coloring Pages!!

U

DUKE

Phonics Series

Preschool:

Kindergarten:

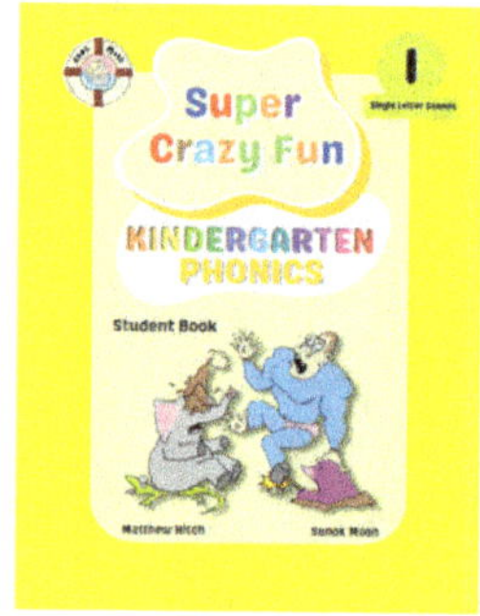    

Elementary School Junior:

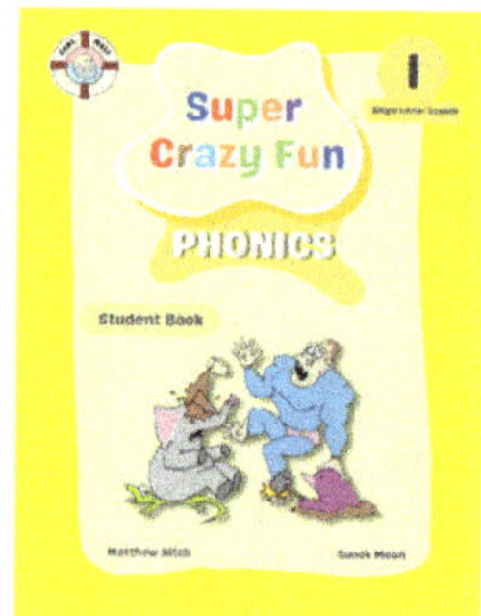 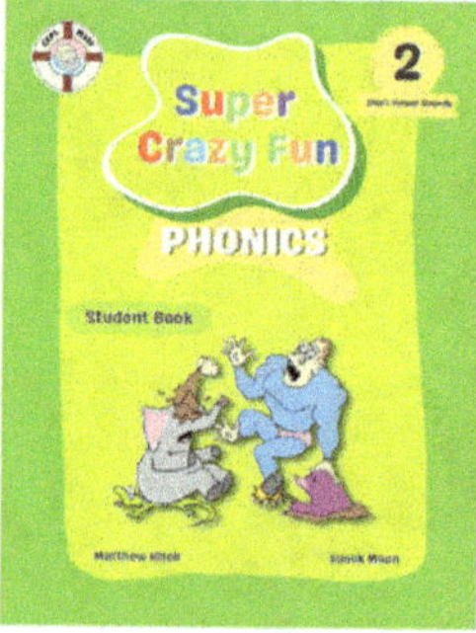 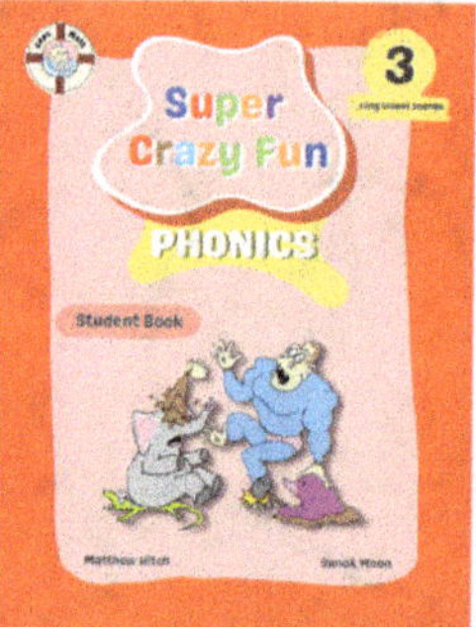  

Elementary School Senior/Remedial:

There's nothing on this page...